Proudly We Hail

Profiles of Public Citizens in Action

Kenneth Lasson

GROSSMAN PUBLISHERS
A Division of The Viking Press   *New York*   *1975*

PROUDLY WE HAIL

First published in 1975 by Grossman Publishers
625 Madison Avenue, New York, N.Y. 10022

Published simultaneously in Canada by
The Macmillan Company of Canada Limited

SBN 670-58018-x

Library of Congress Catalogue Card Number: 74-6641

Printed in U.S.A.

All royalties from the sale of this book will be given to The Center
for Study of Responsive Law, the organization established by Ralph
Nader to conduct research into abuses of the public interest by business and governmental groups. Contributions to further this work are
tax deductible and may be sent to the Center at P.O.B. 19367, Washington, D.C. 20036.

in memory of my father

Acknowledgments

Research Assistants:
Ellen Miller
Anita Rechler

Besides the substantial contributions of Ms. Miller and Ms. Rechler, I wish to acknowledge the valuable advice, assistance, and encouragement rendered by Edgar and Phoebe Berman, Jill Cutler, Ruth Fort, Gale Lawrence, Sylvia Mehlman, and Daniel Sykes, by The Center for Study of Responsive Law, Grossman Publishers, and Loyola College, and by my wife and family.

K.L.

Contents

Prologue

*What is best about this country doesn't
need exaggeration. It needs vigilance.*
                                    —*Bill Moyers*

America is a country continuously struggling for its soul. The richness of its heritage is transcended only by the nobility of its creed, an ongoing commitment to self-determining, self-restrained democracy. Despite the skepticism born of contemporary political and economic turmoil, we still hold to be self-evident the truth it has taken revolutions to articulate: "that all Men are created equal, that they are endowed by their Creator with certain unalienable Rights, that among these are Life, Liberty, and the Pursuit of Happiness."

Yet democracy as a way of life is often accepted intellectually and rejected emotionally. In many other ways there is a dichotomy between what we say and how we act. Deceit runs rampant through the highest levels of government, public servants arrogantly renounce faith in the public's common sense, and the electorate's distrust of elected officials has become pervasive. Much more must be done to make the government responsive to the people; we hide too easily behind the aphorism "it may not be perfect but it's the best so far."

Nevertheless, citizens remain free to vote according to their own choice and disposition. We continue to demand that corruption, no matter how embarrassing to the national character, be brought into the open. Every man, be he President or pauper, is—theoretically—held equal before the law.

The American Paradox goes well beyond simple notions of integrity in government. "Freedom" is still one of our most elusive words. Although it is central to the American consciousness, and for many has presented the opportunity to overcome adversity, for many others—the migrant laborer in California, the sharecropper in Mississippi, the coal miner in West Virginia, the welfare mother in Harlem—deprivation is the yardstick by which freedom is measured. The nation's history is marked with shameful episodes of discrimination against Indians, blacks, Orientals, and Chicanos. Progress in civil rights has often been slow and painful. Some of the disadvantaged are making strides, but their brothers are left trapped in the ghetto. It may be that whites will never understand the larger notion of equality which people of other colors have in mind—a full share of power, responsibility, income, respect—and political philosophers may never resolve the question of whether a system of competitive free enterprise can accommodate our commitment to provide equal opportunity. Real doubt exists whether the country is willing to redistribute income, jobs, and housing in a way that will produce results instead of rhetoric. Much more must be done before our mutual pledge—of lives, fortune, and sacred honor, to secure the blessings of liberty for ourselves and for posterity—becomes more than an eloquently empty promise.

But the fact remains that no other country in the world has ever been faced with—and literally torn itself apart in accepting—so great a challenge to achieve true racial equality. The back of the bus and the rest room for Colored Only are now only symbols of past discrimination. Culturally disadvantaged individuals have become increasingly accomplished; a new-found ethnic pride and awareness is slowly bringing about psychic equality. True freedom, although it may still be more conceptual than real, is guaranteed by a Constitution that is remarkable for its simplicity, visionary in its scope.

There is no doubt that the nation's greatest strength is in its people. Americans live everywhere, come in all colors and all faiths from all parts of the earth, and talk a language entirely their own. The country abounds with Little Italys, Chinatowns, Harlems. Southern drawls and New England twangs bespeak fierce provincialism, yet almost 20 per cent of all Americans change homes every year and millions travel abroad.

The special dynamism of America is reflected on all sides by its pioneers and mechanics, farmers and trade-union workers, inventors, financiers, engineers, and educators who help the nation lead the world in technical innovation. Scientific research and achievement is a magnificent blending of stubbornness, sophistication, and seat-of-the-pants ingenuity. Americans invented the phrase "the sky's the limit": Benjamin Franklin flew a kite and stumbled across original and important principles of electricity; a couple of bicycle repairmen named Orville and Wilbur Wright tested their theories of flight in a foot-square wind box that cost a few dollars to build; the National Aeronautics and Space Administration (having already landed a man on the moon) launched three astronauts to fix an orbiting laboratory with the help of a few old-fashioned but well-placed kicks and hammers. Urban renewal and suburban growth are almost frighteningly constant. Few Americans are without plumbing—or television—and the telephone system is the best anywhere. Opportunities for unfettered communication, both public and private, are virtually boundless.

But being first or biggest or fastest does not always indicate the best kind of progress. Much more must be done to assure peaceful and productive applications of the country's science and technology, because of the enormous implications they carry for the welfare of the world.

There are few other nations in whose history almost any kind of advancement has been so possible—it seems that more people "succeed" in America than anywhere else. One need not be born to gentility to prosper. Social and economic mobility blur class distinctions. Andrew Jackson, to many of his contemporaries a crude, hot-tempered frontiersman and Indian-fighter, rose from a humble background as an orphan to become a prosperous farmer, whose dignity and bearing, thought Daniel Webster, were "more presidential" than those of any of the other candidates of the day; Lincoln was spurred by diligence and determination, not wealth and breeding; Harry Truman, without benefit of a twentieth-century college education, worked his way from haberdasher to President. All American parents may entertain the possibility that their child might some day occupy the nation's highest office.

But the great expectations have their flip side: the ladder is too long from top to bottom, with too many always grouped on the lower rungs. Because of our Protestant-work-ethic attitude about welfare cheaters, our responsiveness to the plight of slum-dwellers is often confused. Materialism and money-mongering have perverted the American Dream into a distasteful myth.

The national character remains, however, extraordinarily adaptable. A 1973 survey of 3000 self-made American businessmen concluded that they were no longer satisfied with the traditional success ethic—that they were seeking instead "the richness of human experience and the rewards inherent in a social reality in which genuine opportunities for self-expression are nearly limitless." The new generation pursues goals beyond the accumulation of financial assets and social status. Americans continue to contribute more to charity than any other people in the world. Our universities seek to change curricula with the changing times. Our dreams are usually realized more fully (though perhaps imperfectly) than those of other nations.

America was once beautiful, from the rugged coasts of New England, across the plains of Kansas and Nebraska, to the beaches of California. Father Andrew White, who sailed with the first boatload of settlers in Maryland, noted in his diary: "in passing through the very thick woods, at every step we tread on strawberries, vines, sassafras, acorns, and walnuts. The soil is dark and not hard, to the depth of a foot, and overlays a rich, red clay. There are lofty trees everywhere, except where the land has been cultivated by a

few persons. Numerous springs furnish a supply of water.
No animals are seen except deer, beaver and squirrels, which
are as large as the hares of Europe. There is an infinite
number of birds of various colors, such as eagles, cranes,
swans, geese, partridges and ducks." And parts of America
are still lovely. Nantucket, Chesapeake Bay, the Shenandoah
Valley, Hilton Head, Saint John National Island. The Ever-
glades of Florida, the hills of Dakota, the flatlands of Texas,
the Great Lakes, the Grand Canyon, the Pacific Northwest.

But for far too long we have strewn our fields with beer
cans and signs, dumped phosphates in the rivers, spilled oil
on the oceans, and poured monoxide into the air. We have
plunged highways through virgin forests and saturated them
with automobiles. We have stripped the land of its verdancy
and poisoned its waters. While the grass roots are assuming
a consciousness of their own, taking hold of *their* vested
interests with renewed efforts to conserve the land's natural
resources, while we have finally begun to question long-
vested capital and to punish polluters, much more direct
action is needed to repair the damage that has already been
done.

America is a country whose culture is exceedingly diver-
sified yet cumulatively distinct. American food is evocative
of Memorial Day, the Fourth of July, and Thanksgiving:
hot dogs, steak, turkey, Maine lobster, Maryland crabcakes,
Kentucky fried chicken, Florida and California oranges,
Idaho baked potatoes, ice-cream sodas, wheatcakes with
syrup, French fries with ketchup, Coca-Cola. There is mulli-
gan stew along the railroad tracks, peanuts and popcorn
at the World Series, a mint julep at the Kentucky Derby,
watermelon at the family picnic. There are also black-eyed
peas and chitlings, gefilte fish and knishes, spaghetti and
pizza, chow mein and won ton soup, baklava and couscous,
and restaurants which specialize in each. Many dishes are
vintage American. A colonial "booke of cookery" suggested

that a midwinter's dinner menu consist of "giblet pie, gravy soup and chicken, roast beef with horseradish and pickles, a tansy with orange, woodcocks on toast, rabbit with savory pudding, roasted turkey and butter apple pie." James Beard still uses recipes passed down by his grandparents who crossed to Oregon in a covered wagon: dried apples and corn, small bits of game impaled on sticks and roasted, vinegar pie ("a practical and tasty solution to the lack of citrus fruits in winter"), and cornmeal cakes and loaves cooked on a griddle.

But despite the fact that Americans enjoy greater variety and abundance than ever before, and are more conscious of calories, quality, and sound nutrition, we also overeat, and our marketplaces are saturated with junk-food adulterated by poorly tested additives. Something is wrong, and must be changed, when farmers are paid not to grow their crops, and poultry producers drown chickens they cannot afford to feed.

There is much that is right—unique, vibrant, diverse—about American culture, when it is not inhibited and over-whelmed by contemporary brutalizations. It is easy to take pride in American art—from the nostalgic precision of Currier and Ives, Thomas Hart Benton, and Grandma Moses, to the character distillations of Norman Rockwell, the abstract expressionism of Jackson Pollock, the archi-tecture of Frank Lloyd Wright, the infinite detail of Andrew Wyeth, and the revolutionary pop of Andy Warhol—which reflects a distinctive vitality, independence, and dimension. The same is true of American music, lilting with Stephen Foster, marching with John Philip Sousa, jiving with Louis Armstrong, and all the shades in between: George Gershwin, Aaron Copland, Leonard Bernstein, Mahalia Jackson, Rodg-ers and Hammerstein, Bob Dylan, Simon and Garfunkel. "Appalachian Spring," *Fiddler on the Roof,* "Sounds of Si-lence." Woodstock and Watkins Glen. The literature of

America is likewise variegated—from Emerson, Whittier, Whitman, Holmes, Melville, Hawthorne, Poe, Pound, and O. Henry, to Fitzgerald, Faulkner, Steinbeck, Frost, Hemingway, Malamud. Here was the motion-picture industry's first home; American film and theater, while often inconsistent in quality, at their best elicit world-wide ovations.

We are not beyond the point, however, where our symphony orchestras must struggle to survive, where airwaves and print media are encumbered with commercialism, and where there remain both subtle and overt forms of censorship.

Excellence in America is perhaps measured most passionately on the playing fields. In 1973 an estimated 100 million people watched or participated in some sort of sporting activity. Statistics and records are a national mania. Baseball, football, basketball, tennis—collegiate and professional—actually any kind of game: chess, polo, lacrosse, bowling, racing, arm wrestling, log-rolling. Athletes become folk heroes (Babe Ruth, Hank Aaron, Willie Mays, Jim Thorpe, Johnny Unitas, Jesse Owens, Wilt Chamberlain, Jack Dempsey, Muhammad Ali, Billie Jean King, Stan Smith, Bobby Jones, Jack Nicklaus). So do horses (Man o' War, Secretariat).

Though love of competition remains indelibly within the American psyche, however, our sporting sense is too often dulled by a "winning is everything" impulse. Big business and high politics have become large parts of sport in this country. Amateurism is colored by hypocrisy.

Through it all, America's sense of humor remains intact. It has always been raucous, slapstick, satirical, irreverent— from Brackenridge and Trumbull, through Buster Keaton and Will Rogers and H. L. Mencken, to Ring Lardner, James Thurber, Ogden Nash, Fred Allen, Bob Hope, Jack Benny, Lenny Bruce, Bill Cosby, Woody Allen, from goldfish-swallowing through telephone-booth stuffing to streaking. We have never lost the essential ability to laugh at ourselves. (Mark Twain on public servants: "Kind of discouragin, it's so hard to find men of so high type of morals that they'll *stay* bought." Jonathan Winters as a modern farmer: "We can't get anythin' from the ground, but the government pays us $25,000 to *watch* it. One of them gummint fellers came down the other day and tole me we couldn't grow cauliflowers here, so we went out to Sears Roebuck and got *plastic* cauliflowers and stuck 'em in the ground—just t' *bug* 'em, see? [*plaintively*] I'd like to farm somethin' just *once*, just for the hell of it. Why the other night some people found out I was a farmer, and I didn't know what t' *say*.")

But perhaps the most revealing aspect of what's right with America is that no other people on earth are as addicted to self-scrutiny, self-criticism, and self-realization. Practically everyone voices a grievance and organizes to fight for rights: minorities for equal opportunity, women for equal status, students to be taken seriously. Peace demonstrators and consumer advocates are as purely American as flag-waving Communist-baiters. All cite the dictum "It's still a free country"—q·ick to invoke the freedoms of religion, speech, press, and assembly, or the guarantees of privacy and due process.

On a bitter cold evening during the height of the Vietnam war thousands of youthful protesters sat huddled against the chill on the steps of the Capitol in Washington. They were singing "The Battle ymn of the Republic," "The Star-Spangled Banner," "America the Beautiful"—and "We Shall Overcome." A veteran of the same war, ravaged by both loyalty and conscience, repudiated his blood-earned decorations by casting them away from his wheel chair in front of the same Capitol.

What, so proudly, do we hail?

Our streets are filled with violence and crime, and too many citizens see fit to take the law into their own hands. Many Americans are leaving the United States in disillusionment, or dropping out with drugs, or losing faith under increasing environmental insults. Material ambitions continue to obscure moral values. Depending on the beholder's current patriotic persuasion, the phrase *what's right with America* conjures up a variety of dissimilar responses: overwhelming arrogance, hopelessly hardened negativism, or starry-eyed naïveté.

There is a certain cogency to each of those vibrations, but each in turn falls short of one of the things most right with America—its capacity for recognizing, and meeting head-on, what's wrong. Our threshold of resignation to existing problems remains exceedingly low: we may say you can't fight City Hall, but we refuse to stop trying.

America—the eloquent dream, the noble heritage, the harsh and struggling reality. That same image which makes immigrants kiss the soil draws passionate cynicism from those who can no longer abide their country's abuse of environment or failure of ethos. These are the extremes. Though the virtues endure upon which the nation was founded, America remains a land of promise and paradox, its natives usually the first to ask how satisfying their own prosperity—or empty their fulfillment.

The models of performance which follow represent some of those individuals and groups who have acted on their capacity to solve problems. They were chosen not to catalogue do-gooders or pronounce endorsements but to applaud the exemplary efforts of Americans who have demonstrated —in creative, efficient, democratic, and innovative ways— that people may indeed regain control over decisions that affect their lives.

It is easy to look at the nation's weaknesses and failures and see a more universal pattern of turmoil and strife. But it is wrong. Life in America is neither a simple reflection of evil impulses nor an apple-pie utopia. As the country continues to grow, there will be new and different causes for animosities and apprehensions. Yet the opportunity to direct that growth—to solve those problems and redress the grievances—is greater here and now than at most other times in the history of the world.

People Acting Alone

*Neither democracy nor effective representation
is possible until each participant in the
group—and this is true equally of a household
or a nation—devotes a measurable part
of his life to furthering its existence.*
—*Lewis Mumford*

Public Citizens

The Quality Controller

In his first fifteen years at the Lockheed Georgia Company, Henry Durham devoutly believed in the company—the only private employer he had ever had—within whose corporate structure he had risen from a $50-a-week dispatcher to a $20,000-a-year production control manager. "What was good for Lockheed was good for the world, as far as I was concerned." Even in August 1969, after he had assumed a managerial position, he had little inclination to suspect deliberate falsification of records and collusion with the Air Force.

Now Durham, described by a journalist as a "kind, soft-spoken man, proud of his home and family, proud of his participation in community affairs," is viewed by many in his home town of Marietta, Georgia, as a public enemy. In 1969, as general department manager in charge of all production-control activities in the flight line and test areas at Lockheed Georgia, he began to discover serious deficiencies in C-5A aircraft upon their arrival from the final assembly department. He soon realized that the defects he was noticing were the products of shabby workmanship and incredibly poor quality control. "The worst and most significant problem was the fact that the C-5A aircraft were missing many thousands of parts—which had, according to Lockheed records, been installed." So Durham took it upon himself to charge that "Lockheed was falsifying completion data in order to fraudulently collect progress payments and to appear to be on schedule."

At first he was reluctant to blow the whistle. "I thought there might have been a flaw in the record-keeping system, or some other type of error. Making sure of my facts, I went to my superiors with the problem—expecting everyone to rush to the rescue. Instead, I was told to shut up. I then issued a series of written reports. Again, I was told to keep quiet and to hide the reports. I refused to heed such an order, and started up the chain of command. I thought surely someone would take action—I just needed to find the right person. I went all the way to the president of the Lockheed Georgia Company and eventually to the chairman of the board. I was rebuffed at every turn. Finally, I was forced into a corner and had to leave."

With little reason for continued loyalty to the company, Durham wrote to eighty-six Senators and Representatives, in each case explaining that he possessed irrefutable proof of "disastrously rotten management," waste, and collusion with the Air Force. He particularly wanted to make the facts known before the vote was taken on the then-pending Lockheed bail-out bill, and implored the legislators to investigate further.

There were sixteen replies to his letters, and all, except one, offered nothing more than sympathy. But news of Durham had reached the ears of A. Ernest Fitzgerald, the Defense Department Deputy for Management Systems in the Air Force, who had exposed cost overruns in the C-5A contract and a general disposition toward wasteful practices in federal procurement. Fitzgerald reported to Senator William Proxmire that he thought Durham was on to something. The ex-Lockheed employee had sent several letters to Proxmire, and finally the Senator invited him to testify before his Subcommittee on Economy in Government, although Durham's appearance was postponed until *after* the $250-million Lockheed-bail-out bill was passed.

Meanwhile, reporter Morton Mintz of *The Washington Post* visited Durham at his home in Marietta, examined the evidence, and wrote a long story that was carried in an Atlanta newspaper. The reaction was immediate—and shockingly vicious. Durham's home came under virtual siege, his family was subjected almost constantly to profane telephone calls and other harassments. Angry callers threatened to burn his house and to kill Durham and his family.

What Henry Durham had disclosed was that his former employers often spent up to twelve times as much for parts and equipment as was actually necessary; that forty-two tons of metal parts had rusted away because they had been left outside in barrels; that Lockheed was paying premium prices and delivery charges on rush orders for parts that were already available at the company itself; that in order to get credit for meeting interim Air Force deadlines, Lockheed's quality-control department would verify in writing that stages of the C-5A were virtually complete, when in fact upward of 1000 parts had still to be installed in the portion in question; that it was common for parts to be installed on one plane to enable it to pass Air Force inspection, only to be removed and installed on another for the same purpose; and that overtime wages had to be paid to complete the jobs in time for the Air Force deadlines.

After Lockheed won its Congressional salvation, Durham testified once again and repeated his charges of gross mismanagement, massive waste, and collusion. He brought along a huge amount of documentation, showing (among other things) vastly overpriced items of common hardware and materials.

Lockheed was invited to tell its side of the story. H. Lee Poore, executive vice president of the Lockheed Georgia Company, declined to respond in detail to Durham's charges but attempted instead to belittle his former role at Lockheed. Senator Proxmire, unimpressed by Poore's response, asked the Government Accounting Office to investigate. The GAO's Atlanta field office did a thorough enough job, but GAO headquarters would not release this report even to the Joint Economic Committee. Durham himself managed to obtain a copy for long enough to make duplications, and he passed one on to Senator Proxmire. The GAO audit was devastating, corroborating nearly every aspect of Henry Durham's charges.

In December 1972, Durham was once again called to a special hearing. Accompanying the invitation was a copy of the Comptroller General's report (entitled "Investigation of Charges Concerning Unsatisfactory Management Practice on the C-5A Aircraft Program at the Lockheed Georgia Company"). Durham was stunned. When he read the document supposedly based on the GAO staff study, he was quick to react: "The report is a whitewash. Important and positive findings and substantiations made by the GAO auditors are omitted, obscured, or distorted." Thus his new testimony before the Joint Economic Committee consisted of a very detailed comparison of the two reports.The Comptroller General did not respond to Durham's charges. The Joint Economic Committee does not intend to investigate further.

Durham remains indignant: "The fact that the Comptroller General of the United States would release a dishonest report calculated to conceal disastrously rotten management and complicity between a large corporation and a powerful government agency cannot and must not be tolerated by the American people. The Comptroller General is supposed to be the chief watchdog for Congress and *therefore also of the people*. It is strange that a man can practically destroy himself and his family trying to help his country, while those who participate in corruption and dishonesty and the rape of the federal treasury go scot-free and live the good life.

"I am gravely concerned about the future. There is a moral and ethical sickness that threatens to destroy the country. It seems that honesty and integrity are no longer principles to live by or govern by. But those are the principles which guide my life and this fight. I strongly feel that people should place self-interest aside and stand up for honesty and integrity, regardless of the consequences."

Above all, Henry Durham would hope that his actions encourage others to step forward with disclosures of corruption or dishonesty. "I am more determined than ever. I will never give up."

As Durham wrote in one of his letters to Senator Proxmire: "I do not want to think I am just another disgruntled employee out to get vengeance. I had a very good record at Lockheed and have data to prove it. It's just that I made up my mind to fight the malignancy because it represents the kind of thing I am against. What will America come to if we allow people, groups or companies to violate principles of integrity, decency, honor, and business ethics? It is past time for every American who gives a damn to stand up and become involved."

The Auto Mechanic

Unnecessary and fraudulently inspired automobile repairs cost Americans $25 billion per year—an average of $250 for each of the 100 million cars on United States highways. But the lemon-owner is frequently caught in a squeeze: "too dependent on my tin lizzy to give it up," as one man said, "but too frustrated with lousy service to keep it." In the absence of adequate public transportation there are no alternatives for the aggrieved car-owner except to whistle an expensive tune as his jalopy is being towed away and patched up.

Drivers in Riverdale, Maryland, however, are luckier than most. They are served by a "public-interest mechanic" named Patrick Goss, who actually says things like "Consumers are being taken day in and day out by unscrupulous or incompetent mechanics; the worst part is that not only are we trusting our wallets and our cars to these people, we're trusting our lives."

Goss speaks from experience. Until a few years ago he worked in the most fraudulent of repair shops and learned every gyp tactic the bilkers could devise. The whole business bothered him. There were no restrictions on who was hired, no requests for references, no standards of competence, and no incentives to learn the right way. "In most places, mechanics do the job and the customer is the test pilot."

His concern about the high cost of shoddy repairs first surfaced while Goss was conducting a training course for a manufacturer of electronic testing equipment. Then he read a book called *What to Do with Your Bad Car: An Action Manual for Lemon Owners* (which he now sells to his customers) and emerged with the hope that "if we know what the problems are and why they plague us, we can effectively bring about change within the auto industry—if they know we won't buy junk, perhaps they won't make junk." Now, from the country's first "public-interest gasoline station"— Pat's Gulf and Diagnostic Service—he advises both consumer attorneys and the county's Consumer Protection Commission, and teaches classes in basic auto repairs. In addition, Goss appears on numerous radio and television programs to preach his own brand of gospel, and has written three books on auto repair. He pays his own expenses for travel, consulting, printing, and preparing class materials.

In his basic course ("Gyp Tactics I"), Goss compares what should be done with what often happens in engine tune-ups, battery service, tire inspections, fan-belt replacement, and repairs of suspension, exhaust, and braking systems. The class actually started as one in automobile mechanics, but the professor soon found his students more interested in learning how to avoid being taken. "People want to know what strange sounds mean, and what to instruct the mechanic. Once they understand how their cars work, what makes them run, they're not such easy marks. If a garage says they need a brake job, they want to know if they really need one." The introductory course (two hours per week for five weeks) also teaches how to make simple repairs.

One favorite gyp tactic Goss takes pleasure in exposing is the racket involving bogus starters. "One guy used to brag that he made over a thousand dollars from a one-dollar can of black spray-paint. All he did was repaint the old starter motor, put it back in, and charge the customer forty to fifty dollars for a new motor." Another popular and equally blatant fraud happens with front-end jobs. "A crafty mechanic, by turning a wheel in, can make it look as though it's dangerously loose. However, the front wheel will be usable when it's turned, because the idler arm is beyond its center axis. This doesn't mean anything is wrong. The wheel should be checked when it is straight."

Goss inspects cars as a good doctor examines his patients. After a thorough checkup—including electronic, mechanical, and road tests—he evaluates for each customer the results and indicates safety hazards, necessary repairs, and adjustments that may be delayed. A money-back guarantee accompanies all his work; mistakes, which are rare, are corrected at no charge.

Mechanics who make the wrong repairs are a personal peeve for Goss. "It's not just the rip-offs—they are a small portion of the owner's problem. It's the incompetency. Many mechanics have no idea how to diagnose a problem, much less fix it. If there's something wrong in the electrical system they won't know if it's the alternator, voltage regulator, or battery cable—and they'll sell you each in turn until something works." He doubts that most mechanics know what they are doing with electronic testing equipment. "The tests are no better than the person operating them. The machine can't weigh the differences between something inoperative and something you can let slide for a time. Besides, most diagnostic centers also sell parts. That can be a tricky conflict of interest."

To reduce fraud and eliminate the incompetents, Goss actively advocates the testing and licensing of all mechanics. In order to practice the trade, a mechanic would have to demonstrate that he understands what needs to be done, and that he is capable of implementing what he understands. "Licensing, accompanied by strong penalties and aggressive enforcement, is the only way people with no experience can be stopped from experimenting with other people's money and safety." To this end Goss has submitted a comprehensive proposal to the Prince Georges (Maryland) County Council, as well as to the state legislature.

Goss's outspoken position has not brought him the universal appreciation of his colleagues in the business. There have been threatening phone calls and (after a particularly strong television program) a few smashed windows. At one point the Gulf Oil Company chose not to renew his lease. "The official reason was that my gasoline sales were too low. But they told me, off the record, it was because I was too controversial." When that happened his students and friends contacted the media, and a short time later he was invited to Baltimore by Gulf executives; they did not talk directly about the lease, but slipped the comment that "You have an awful lot of friends out there and we've heard from every one of them." In a few days a new lease arrived.

Goss finds it disturbing that so few mechanics have followed his example. For him, good consumerism is good business, and good business pays dividends in forms other than money.

The Environmental Strategist

Hazel Henderson is a British-born New Yorker who well remembers "killer fog"—a noxious mixture of stagnant air and industrial poisons which was blamed for 4000 deaths related to respiratory diseases. Upon her arrival in Manhattan, in 1956, she saw what had become depressingly familiar: tremendous amounts of pollution that New Yorkers had come to accept as an inevitable aspect of modern life. From that moment on, Hazel Henderson dedicated herself to a cause, and has since become a deft and articulate spokeswoman for antipollution and public-interest forces not only in New York but around the country.

Her education as an activist has not been easy. First, she wrote to local officials, government agencies, and radio and television executives about New York's pollution problems. Some satisfaction came when the major radio and television commentators began to announce the daily air-pollution index, bringing the potential crisis to the attention of a large and previously unaware audience. City Councilman Robert A. Law responded with an invitation for Ms. Henderson to join other angry constituents in a meeting at his office, where in the fall of 1964 a group calling itself Citizens for Clear Air was established. With the voluntary help of advertising man Carl Ally, a campaign to educate New Yorkers to the hazards of air pollution was launched on television, radio, and in print. Within two years there were 24,000 members of the organization. Early in its history, the CCA sent speakers to parent-teacher associations and civic groups, testified before legislative committees, and held dozens of rallies and meetings—all of which contributed substantially to the passage by the New York City Council in 1966 of a tough air-pollution law.

Hazel Henderson's goal is at once simple and immense: to improve the environment by making huge corporations and industries more responsive to law and society. She quickly discovered the most frustrating part of being informed: not knowing how to implement her concern. So she learned to play the games of power. ("The citizen begins to understand that he must do the same thing as the industrial lobbyist or pressure groups, that he, too, must organize.") But she soon found that, while corporations organize as part of the day's work, citizens must operate with minimal funds and after normal business hours.

Fighting the difficulties of recruiting disinterested people, signing petitions, running mimeographs, holding meetings, writing letters, Hazel Henderson became a strategist, pamphleteer, lobbyist, and lecturer. In one of her more effective speeches (which has since been put into the Congressional Record by Senator Edmund S. Muskie), she explained firsthand the problems of becoming an informed citizen, described the intangible obstacles to overcoming the "powers of pollution." One of them is meeting the argument of *expertise*: industry and government often suggest that the citizen is not qualified to make important decisions because he does not have the necessary information. But the same bureaucracies deny to the public the essential data (and the advertising budgets) which are available to "the experts" —the researchers, the lobbyists, the public-relations men. An inhibiting factor is frequently the sheer *size* of large corporate polluters in a given area. Still another difficulty is that of persuading citizen groups not only to push for passage and enforcement of new laws but also to act as watchdogs, assuring that powerful business interests do not try to obtain special dispensations from regulatory agencies.

Hazel Henderson now speaks and writes extensively on

the growing conflict between traditional economics and ecological concerns. She has traveled the globe, from Australia and Japan to Africa and Europe, persuading fellow citizens to learn about and organize for consumer and environmental protection. She believes in the American system, and also that "capitalism can be modified to serve new needs." An associate of the faculty Seminar on Technology and Social Change at Columbia University, a member of the board of directors for four public-interest organizations (the Council on Economic Priorities, the Institute for the Study of Economic Systems, the Public Interest Economics Center, and the Institute for Public Transportation), an advisory board member of the Environmental Action Foundation and the Council on Population and Environment, and a Fellow of the Scientists Institute for Public Information, her involvement is not necessarily born of pure altruism. "I just do these things because I think they need doing. My greatest pleasure comes from seeing how individuals grow and become autonomous by way of involvement in civic activities."

The Discrimination Fighter

Julius Hobson likes to quote poetry; he's especially fond of some lines from Countee Cullen, which he feels would fit well if anyone ever decided to do his biography:

> Once, riding in old Baltimore,
>   Heart-filled, head-filled with glee,
> I saw a Baltimorean
>   Keep looking straight at me.
>
> Now I was eight and very small,
>   And he was no whit bigger;
> And so I smiled, but he poked out
>   His tongue, and called me "Nigger."
>
> I saw the whole of Baltimore
> From May until December;
> Of all the things that happened there
>   That's all that I remember.

"Right now," says Hobson, "you would have to walk for days in Baltimore or Washington before you would find someone to come right out and call you nigger. It just isn't done—it's not the gentlemanly thing. The nature of the beast of discrimination has changed; there is less open friction between the races. The average man on the street no longer takes the law into his own hands. There has been a change in terms of blacks getting jobs, blacks getting higher positions. What frightens me about what is going on in the country right now is that blacks, particularly young blacks, are duplicating the white man's mistakes. The whole thrust toward separatism is a bad move. But I know from my youth that it takes a tremendous effort to throw off hate.

I've found that my shoulders are just not broad enough to carry around all that hate."

Hobson is a citizen-activist of the first order, with an impressive record of public service dedicated to overcoming racism, injustice, and inequality. His greatest efforts, and acknowledged contributions, have been in the area of employment discrimination; his most gratifying fight has been the struggle to get all blacks employed by the government into jobs commensurate with their abilities.

Hobson's methodology runs the gamut from private influence to public boycott. When he began in 1960, "a black salesclerk was as rare as a white crow" in downtown Washington, D.C. By the time he had finished, there were close to 5000 blacks working in retail positions. From 1960 until 1964, as president of the local Congress on Racial Equality (CORE) chapter, Hobson organized picket lines around some of the capital's largest stores—Lansburgh's, Woodward & Lothrop, Safeway, Bonds, Woolworth's, and Hahn Shoes. Within a relatively short time, much of the rampant racial discrimination in hiring had been dissolved.

His records in the areas of public housing, education, health, and transportation are equally impressive. *Hobson v. Hansen* in 1967 resulted in the outlawing of teacher segregation and the differential distribution of books and supplies, setting an example for many other school systems across the country. A Hobson-led march on the District Building (where 4500 people demonstrated) sparked passage of the present housing ordinance desegregating all apartment buildings in Washington. Another demonstration yielded the integration of hospital facilities and services.

Hobson's self-generated public citizenship extended even further afield. He was an active member of the Emergency Committee on the Transportation Crisis, protesting freeways that were to have cut right through local communities. He was active as well in protests against bus-fare increases that were seen as discriminatory to blacks and the poor. He gave leadership to the D.C. Statehood Party—the fledgling political organization dedicated to self-government for citizens of the District of Columbia. He has been in and out of court enforcing the famous Wright Decree establishing new guidelines for equality of educational opportunity.

"President Kennedy gave a lot of lip service to the question of the poor having the right to participate in and make decisions affecting their lives. But the poor people didn't get a damn thing out of the poverty program. It really turned out to be kind of a job exchange for sociologists and economists. If you could write a paper on how it feels to be hungry you could get a job. The good thing was that the Kennedy and Johnson administrations created a politically aware group of people who started thinking in terms of their rights. In other words, we got a society of welfare mothers who were not about to get in a damn soup line again and say, 'Thank you boss, I'm glad to get this.' They created a political awareness all over the country. Any ghetto that you go into, whether it be Chicano, black, or Indian, there is an alertness and awareness by the people who live there. People started to read, they started to talk." Hobson continues the struggle—testifying before Congress, writing, teaching, serving on the Washington, D.C. Board of Education, filing class actions (lawsuits on behalf of a large group)—but above all he dedicates himself to the full and free exercise of good citizenship. He is perfectly sincere when he says, "I think a man or woman owes an obligation to his fellow man to make a contribution to the world, to eliminate the kind of unhappiness and the kind of suffering that goes on. A country is not a geographical boundary, or a flag with some stripes. I believe that I owe a fellow human being the kind of relationship which will keep him free from fear, make him happy, or contribute to his tomorrow."

Julius Hobson is a different kind of hero, but still one

from the heart of America. He has been through it all, and confesses nothing more than to "love poets, flowers, the sunrise and sunset, and the people who write about daffodils." His favorite people are "men who were pioneers or heroes in the struggle for freedom"—like Frederick Douglass, who said, "If there is no struggle, there is no progress. Those who profess to freedom and yet deprecate agitation are men who want crops without plowing. Power concedes nothing without demand. It never did and it never will."

"I've always contended," says Hobson, "that people like myself, activists, are taken from circumstances and surroundings. I'm like a man who's in a boat that's sinking and I've got to bail to keep from sinking. It seems to me that any black man born under the same circumstances that I was born under, and was living in, had no choice but to fight or die. I had to bail all the time.

The Road Watcher

Perhaps the greatest impact on highway-safety legislation in the United States has been registered neither by government nor industry but by a poorly educated, self-employed television repairman using his spare time and life savings.

It started about ten years ago for Joseph Linko. Driving his truck on the Cross Bronx Expressway in New York, he noticed two concrete stubs protruding from a partial shoulder by the side of the road. He knew that more than a year earlier the sign they once held had been knocked over, and saw that the stanchions were obviously serving no useful purpose

"If a car was forced off the road at that spot, the occupants wouldn't stand a chance. So I began to wonder, are we spending great sums of money for new highways with the same kind of booby traps?" Wondering also why neither city nor state had removed the stubs, he bought a camera for $25 and took a picture of the hazard. Then, "everywhere I went my common sense showed me something worse, so I started taking other photographs." In little more than a year he had accumulated some 300 slide pictures of the perils designed into highways.

At first he tried alerting newspapers to the dangers he came across every day; several challenged his expertise ("Are you a traffic engineer?"), few felt his information newsworthy. His letters to city and state highway departments went unanswered. Although he felt foolish taking the slides by the side of the road, and although they were costing him 25 cents apiece, he persisted. ("If I had been married, I probably wouldn't have had the time.")

After one particular hazard he had warned against caused a fatal accident, Linko wrote to Governor Nelson Rockefeller. That deficiency was corrected, but no others. The American Association of State Highway Officials expressed interest in his work, but little more than academic attention was paid to the deficiencies themselves. At the suggestion of a friend (William Toth, professor of Safety Education at New York University), Linko wrote to Congress. Again, no response.

Finally, in 1967—a full five years after he had begun his private crusade—the House Subcommittee on Federal Aid to Highways became aware of the existence of Joseph Linko, and he was asked to testify at hearings on the nation's highway situation. "I went to Washington with my slides and notes and hoped they would understand what I was trying to do. I'm not an engineer, but what I was saying was just common sense."

Linko testified—at first uncertainly and then with considerable confidence that he was making his point. He told the Congressmen his free-lance investigation had led him to conclude that either highway and traffic engineers didn't know what they were doing or, if they did know, no one else had cared enough to challenge them. He detailed his astonishment at the numbers and kinds of serious hazards that littered the roadsides of some of the busiest and newest thoroughfares in the New York area, claiming their toll in human life every day.

Among the specific dangers, Linko pointed out that:

—Guardrail ends were spearing vehicles that swerved from the roadway, sometimes causing several feet of guardrail to intrude into the passenger compartment and resulting in horrible mutilating deaths.

—Heavy concrete sign stanchions and utility poles

were being installed within a couple of feet of the roadway edge and left exposed.

—Concrete and steel sign supports were being erected
and left exposed in the gore area of freeway exits, where
statistical evidence shows run-off-the-road incidents occur
four times more frequently than elsewhere along a freeway.

—Rigid light poles in extremely vulnerable spots were
being hit, often causing death and injury, and replaced
time and time again in the same fashion.

Linko helped demonstrate that a wealth of specialized
research information—and common sense—could be applied
more effectively to the crash dynamics that involve the individual, the vehicle, and the roadway. His evidence was
replete with photographs and straightforward commentary.

At one point, he showed the subcommittee a slide of a
guardrail that was pointed like an arrow toward the
approach end of a concrete bridge. He said that motorists
had been "chipping away on this thing" for a long time and
that he knew it was destined to cause trouble. Eight months
after he had taken the picture, a mother and two of her
children were killed when the rail deflected their car into
the bridge abutment; four days later, another person was
killed at the same spot. Only after his letter to the Governor
was remedial action taken. "If the guardrail had been
installed properly and secured to the abutment, a car would
slide by and continue on its way. But when you touched this
one, the way it was, it just moved back and you hit the abutment head on. Thousands of people are being killed and
injured every year running into abutments, telephone poles,
and light poles. All you have to do is read the papers. And
we are doing brand new jobs just like this."

The subcommittee was impressed. Using a booklet prepared with the help of Linko's pictures, it proceeded to lambast the highway builders and called for the avoidance of new hazards and the elimination of existing ones. Linko felt temporarily vindicated and proud of his efforts: "I proved that ninety percent of the unnecessary death traps that lined our new state and interstate highways had nothing to do with extra money. By using plain common sense, most of these death traps could have been designed out of the new roads, and in a few cases a few dollars more could have saved complete rebuilding of the highways, at today's inflated prices. The credit should be given to George Kopecky and the subcommittee staff, and to Congressman John A. Blatnik, the chairman. They had the power to correct, because ninety percent of road funds were paid by the federal government. Still, I wasn't able to fight the government—they held public hearings and contacted *me* to see the slides."

Linko's personal study was not limited to examination of the hazards. He had suggestions for safety improvements in almost every category of the dangers he had documented, including replacement of iron supports with aluminum poles (just as sturdy but which crumple more easily on impact), placement of signs on the side of walls or near natural embankments or at bridge abutments (leaving narrow shoulders open for emergency steps), and removal of unnecessary obstacles.

As a result of his testimony, the Department of Transportation began to require compliance with higher safety standards in the design and construction of highways as a condition for receiving federal aid. It was discovered that about a third of the fatal accidents on the interstate system are single-vehicle, run-off-the-road collisions, with many of the cars involved striking one or more fixed objects. Said Congressman Blatnik: "Regardless of the reasons why a driver may leave the paved portion of a high-speed highway, road-

side areas should be sufficiently clear of obstruction to give
him an opportunity to regain control . . . a reasonable chance
of survival."

Other members of Congress who heard Linko's testimony
were moved to look beyond the highway dangers themselves
and to ask exactly who was accountable. They pointed out
the tragic irony of the highway booby traps, that the
engineering answers were known years ago, and that it
would have cost less human suffering as well as less money
to have avoided the hazards when the roads were built.
Millions of dollars had been wasted on unnecessary signs and
guardrails and trees planted too close to the road; energy-
absorbing materials could have been placed on abutments
and at high-accident locations.

Linko's satisfaction from the 1967 hearings was short-
lived. Although his efforts have caused a revolution in the
design of American highways, many of the existing hazards
remain uncorrected and continue to take their toll in deaths
and injuries. When he looks back on his activities over the
past ten years, there is a touch of bitterness mixed with
the frustration.

"No one would listen in my efforts to fight the city, state,
and federal governments when they were building the tens
of thousands of unnecessary booby traps along our new
state and interstate highways. Over the years I spent all my
savings—twenty, twenty-five thousand dollars or more, I
don't know—this in cash. The time of many years' work
comes to a lot more. All my efforts failed. The government
agencies did not act, the newspapers didn't print these
wrongs, because this is the way we were always building our
roads. One year before the hearings the Automobile Association of America saw three hundred of my color slides and
failed to call me back after I had showed them the design
errors. I was the only one fighting for this cause in the beginning, and I had no highway experience. I was using plain com-

mon sense to fight the highway engineers and governments. Because I had to make a living, I used to spend four hours a day and most of Saturday and Sunday taking the pictures. The rest of the time I had to do my TV work. I could never follow up on things that needed to be done. Because no one would help, it took years to gather evidence to prove that the government was on a full-scale hazard-building program, with the aid of federal money. I saw New York, New Jersey, and Connecticut building these booby traps into new roads. The subcommittee then checked all over the United States and found out that all the other states were building death traps, too. We were wasting billions of dollars of taxpayers' money needlessly. Seventeen thousand people were dying every year, and millions were being hurt and crippled for life, for no good reason. Also billions of dollars in property damage was going down the drain every year. The public officials and safety departments, engineers, highway designers, inspectors, insurance companies, and all the rest who could have spoken up for the motorists' cause didn't; they were on the city, state, and federal payrolls. I was the only one in my area speaking up, and I had to use my own money.

"No one in Congress wants to take a stand on these issues. What good are laws when Congress knows they are being broken and they fail to act and use the penalty? The states are guilty of criminal negligence; thousands of motorists die because of their errors and negligence. It's in the Congressional Record on the 1967 hearings. The laws they are breaking are in the book. I read this book, so I know."

Despite his obvious frustration, Linko continues to struggle for corrections of the hazards he sees every day, and to make suggestions on how others can do the same.

"Any lawyer or citizen who builds a case against the government and wins should be paid the going rate for investigative work and court time. I was poor to begin with, but because of my work on highway safety I have no savings and will have to rely on my veteran's pension—a hundred dollars a month. I fought for the people's rights, and I'm really punished money-wise. Since no one asked me to do this, I can't complain. I myself have made safety of the roads my personal business. I know I could make the roads a hundred-per-cent safer in my area if I could work full time for this cause, without having to worry about supporting myself.

"But there might be fair ways to pay the citizen his expenses and a bonus for his reward, at no cost to the governments. I suggest the money could come from fines—of government officials and civil-service employees who failed to do their duty or made errors or were incompetent. Maybe all government workers should be bonded so that when they mess up, the people can get paid by the bonding office. Until something like this is done, the citizen could never be expected to act, even though it's his duty for good government. We can't afford to hire thousands of inspectors, but there are millions of citizens who can do the job free for the government if they could get the fine money.

"It's hard to fight governments. Somehow, everyone feels he has something to lose because the government can investigate him. Small, unimportant things they might have done worry people, and they say to themselves, Why rock the boat? Someone else will do it. But the job never gets done. Actually, we need a special group of lawyers checking the government's daily operations full time."

Thus Joseph Linko remains a public citizen of the highest order, a layman simply concerned by the dangers built into the roads of his native city and aware of common-sense solutions that can be applied there and elsewhere. With no outside encouragement, his efforts have led to much more careful design in highways—and undoubtedly to a large number of saved lives.

The Creative Newsperson

"If the next generation of Americans enjoys a cleaner and more beautiful world," read a Louisville *Courier-Journal* editorial, "one hopes that fair tribute will be paid to Mary Moss and others who did not stand idly by while we slowly gagged to death on the pollution of our air, water and earth."

The woman who won that unusual praise is Mary Moss, WAVE-TV's Environmental Reporter in Louisville. What the newspapers were editorializing was not only her ability "to bring to life the technical and complicated story of pollution in that community" but a special program she had written for school children in Kentucky called the *ABC's of Environment*. Now national distribution will let children everywhere benefit from it.

"The *ABC*'s is somewhat an index to my personality," Mary Moss admits. "If I have an obsession, it is for people to know and understand the way it really is. We have been so abused by the institutions that were meant to serve us; the best service we can perform is to inform ourselves, so that those institutions will improve."

Mary Moss has offered more of herself than mere words in order that others might have the benefits of clean air, nonpolluted water, and a better environment. Moving to Louisville from New York City, where she worked for the United Nations, she was recruited to the "clean-air cause" by a young physician (who went on to become the Mayor of Louisville). She was a novice in the field, and up against an industrially oriented state establishment whose interests in coal are strong. She joined the Board of Action for Clean

Air to educate herself on how citizens could testify at public hearings for clean-air standards.

"Hundreds of people were organized in the seminars and training sessions at the University of Louisville, in what had to be the most arduous period of my life; what we can proudly say is that Jefferson County, Kentucky, got stricter standards than the State as a whole. By that time I had convinced myself that individuals made the difference."

She had also learned the importance of accurate information. By now a wife and mother, Mary Moss set her sights on the most effective way to reach the largest numbers. Her goal was to convince a major television station that coverage of subjects concerning environmental or consumer problems was essential. She was told that commercial stations wouldn't buy such a "touchy" program, but she impressed the CBS affiliate in Louisville with a series of reports on water, solid waste, and the automobile. Nine spots appeared on regular newscasts, each dealing with how a defined environmental problem was reflected in Kentucky.

These won her a full-time news-reporting job as environmental reporter with the local NBC affiliate. Mary Moss's frame of reference had expanded and her consumer and environmental news was being heard on radio and television three times weekly. She describes her desk at the station as an "over-ground clearing house," but every call and letter receives an answer. Many of her best news stories come from distressed citizens. Often government officials, frustrated themselves by the system, willingly tell all. "Many are people wanting me to know they've solved a problem. They get equal time in my book, because they're doing something."

Mary Moss credits her station with a lot of what has gone right. "They've never inhibited me in any way. That's more than you can say about many stations in this country which would rather stay as far from the fire as possible. I don't deny that some of my reports raise some smoke—but my job is to be certain that the information is correct, whether it makes certain parties uncomfortable or not."

One of her news stories, on airport workers without adequate ear protection, brought them protective headgear within hours. An old elm tree shading a church, scheduled to be cut down for a wider road, still stands. An amusement park which dumped its sewage into the Ohio River has been cleaned up. "Once information is public, and the right people are aware, things change."

Mary Moss was also active some years ago in helping to found a citizens' action coalition in Louisville called Strategies for Environmental Control. It was through this group that she put her *ABC's of Environment* into the Louisville and Jefferson County school systems. With the help of a grant from the National Endowment for the Arts, the program was made into a filmstrip with narration and original music. "There are no sunsets and happy music endings. From A for Air to Z for Zero Population Growth, it sells not a point of view but a view of many points." The *Courier-Journal* called it a "smash hit."

Now involved in a number of activities which confront environmental problems through the media, Mary Moss feels more certain than ever that institutions, whether governmental or corporate, "can be made to work for people the way they'd like them to work."

"It is the individual's obligation to himself not to permit institutions to become indifferent to the people they were meant to serve. Restructured positively, it is the individual's fault if apathy permits this deterioration. Individuals have the capacity to spark the interest and concern of others to change things for reasons other than economic gain.

"Institutions do not necessarily go on being indifferent. Often their reactions are blanketed. For example, an oil company might hire an environmental expert to show its concern publicly. However, their hiring is a chink in the wall. In the same way, commercial stations which depend on advertising for their profit would not welcome a situation which would demean that source of revenue. However, they are also required to service their public locally and to perform in a way which proves to the Federal Communications Commission that their license should be renewed. Hiring an environmental reporter may be a double-edged sword, but, when they do it, there is an act in the right direction nevertheless. Also, it is an old story that the ethics involved in news reporting should prevent interference. At least, this has been so in my case."

Public Servants

The Insurance Commissioner

"That should shake the bastards up a bit," said Herbert S. Denenberg, then Pennsylvania's feisty insurance commissioner, after a taped television interview during which he had lashed out at the insurance companies, lawyers, doctors, and hospitals for contributing to exorbitant medical costs.

It was not an uncharacteristic performance. From the moment Denenberg took office in January 1971 until he resigned in 1974 to wage an unsuccessful campaign for the U.S. Senate, he made news. Challenging the legal, medical, and insurance establishments with a zealot's fervor, he has been overwhelmingly successful in his primary mission—to make the insurance industry responsible to the real needs of the public.

One result of his efforts has been that Pennsylvanians are now more educated than most Americans to health-care costs —and rip-offs—among them these hard facts:

—Identical life-insurance coverage can vary as much as 300 per cent from one company to another.

—Some 2 million unnecessary surgical operations are performed in the United States each year.

—Group auto insurance could slash premiums 10 per cent to 20 per cent.

His actions rendered Denenberg anathema to special-interest groups. In 1972, both the Pennsylvania Medical Society and the Pennsylvania Association of Trial Lawyers demanded that he be fired, and the Insurance Foundation of Pennsylvania, the industry's chief lobby in the state, issued a similar denouncement.

47

Denenberg's flamboyance, however, has made him exceedingly popular with the consumers of Pennsylvania. A respected poll placed him at the top of a list of all public figures in the state in terms of "trust and confidence." (Governor Milton Shapp, who appointed him, was said by some to be the first state chief executive remembered most of all for his insurance commissioner.) This is underscored by political irony of the first magnitude, since the office of insurance commissioner is as unlikely a place from which to attack the industry as a convention hall full of insurance underwriters.

Since the 1920s, when state regulation of insurance practices began, the insurance commissions have often appeared to be more responsive to the needs of organized industry pressure groups than to scattered grievances expressed by consumers, however vociferous they may be. Denenberg is candid: "The regulators and the regulated are too cozy. Personnel are interchangeable; stints as government regulators are internships for lawyers looking toward lucrative careers in industry. About forty per cent of present insurance commissioners across the country have had previous employment with the industry, and former commissioners line the executive suites of insurance companies. All too often, the public goes unrepresented."

Denenberg holds the view, and was not afraid to act on it, that most regulators are content to twiddle their thumbs while invoking the general rule not to make a decision unless one is absolutely necessary. Regulatory laws are usually insufficient to accomplish their avowed purpose; even potentially effective legislation is often emasculated by conservative judiciaries. Lawmakers, moreover, are frequently beholden to the very interests they ostensibly seek to regulate.

The powers of the Pennsylvania Insurance Commissioner —including the right to determine what insurance policies can be sold in the state, and to approve or disapprove

requests for changes in coverage, benefits, and premiums—
do not differ significantly from those of other state insurance commissioners. It was the way he made use of such
powers which put Denenberg's stand above the ordinary.

The commissioner's mandate from Governor Shapp was to
transform the insurance department into a consumer-oriented operation. Denenberg proceeded to hire a press secretary and hold conferences with the media, not only to draw
attention to his ideas but to gain public support through the
generation, disclosure, and dissemination of information. His
theme: "Until insurance becomes a topic of breakfast-table
conversation throughout Pennsylvania, nothing will get
done."

The way the Pennsylvania Insurance Department handled
a proposed local increase in Blue Cross rates should be a
model for like-minded consumer groups and regulatory agencies around the country. A few weeks after Denenberg took
office, Blue Cross of Philadelphia asked for a $73-million rate
increase—the largest in Pennsylvania's history. The rate
hike was justified, claimed Blue Cross, by the fact that hospital costs were increasing as much as 20 per cent annually.
The department categorically refused to authorize any
increase whatsoever—until Blue Cross would agree to
undertake various stipulated reforms and economies. Five
days of hearings on the matter, carried live by public television, called even more attention to rampant waste and inefficiency. Denenberg made the hearings the most lively television program in Pennsylvania, dropping bombshells with
temerity, ordering Blue Cross to renegotiate its existing contracts with participating hospitals, and announcing thirty-
three cost-saving guidelines by which health-delivery reforms
could be implemented. Finally, in order to establish clear-cut
consumer control, he called for a full-scale revision of the
bylaws and articles of Blue Cross. "There was no sense in
pumping money into that hospital system," he reminisces

now with satisfaction, "without demanding a little quality and efficiency in return."

Blue Cross was eventually granted approximately one-eighth of its original request. Little more than a year and a half after the drama began, front-page headlines announced that the rate of inflation of hospital costs for Philadelphians had been checked. Blue Cross premiums would increase by only $9.6 million. Subscribers had been saved at least $65 million a year.

Once reforms were implemented in Philadelphia, the department proceeded to apply them state-wide, still abiding by pragmatic principles that may be easily followed by others seeking similar reforms:

—Identify and clarify the local problem. Understand that the government has limited resources and personnel, and that there must be a conscious decision on how to get the most bank out of the regulatory buck.

—Collect the facts. Fact-raking is valuable to the public and astounds the media. There is no need for muckraking (although indeed the two processes are often the same).

—Publicize the facts. Naming names, prices, and premiums is the only way to reach the man in the street.

—Use leverage. Government often has more power than it can use, but lacks the will to use it.

In short, Denenberg and his department helped to demystify the complex questions of insurance, as well as exercising the legal authority of the commission.

In addition, by issuing clear and simple consumer guides to insurance buying, the Pennsylvania Insurance Department hopes to save consumers additional billions of dollars. "Shoppers Guides" to surgery, dentistry, hospitals, auto insurance, and life insurance, among others, have been published and many more are in the works. Their impact has been immense. "Our list of the ten highest cost companies," said Denenberg, "is the business equivalent of the FBI's Ten Most Wanted List. The public jumps on them, insurance agents jump on them, policyholders jump on them, security analysts jump on them. They just can't survive. Many companies have already lowered premiums as a result of our guides. We also listed ten companies which used gimmick life-insurance policies, such as confusing contracts that made price comparisons virtually impossible. Nine out of ten companies almost immediately withdrew their gimmick policies, and the tenth is now out of the market for all practical purposes. By conventional regulatory procedures it would have taken five years and a platoon of lawyers to get rid of these gimmicks—but the power of publicity knocked them out virt ally overnight. And it was all done with a little booklet that cost about ten cents apiece to print."

The Shoppers Guides have purposely not been copyrighted, and permission to reprint them has readily been granted so that other government and consumer groups can easily follow suit. More than ten other state insurance departments have followed Pennsylvania's lead with their own guides. The insurance booklets suggest other possibilities, such as the guide to health facilities published by the state health department, or one to banking services by the state banking department, or to clothing and food from departments of commerce and agriculture, to buying stocks, automobiles, and homes. The list may be as long and broad as the consumers' need and right to be informed. Citizens themselves could start rating insurance commissioners, banking regulators, attorneys general, legislators, and other public servants. Their evaluations of voting records and over-all performance would be important companions to consumer purchasing guides.

Other activities undertaken by the Pennsylvania Insurance Department likewise set worthy examples. The department drafted legislation (now law) to eliminate the requirement that a majority of the Blue Shield Board be doctors. It initiated a plan to provide basic property insurance to all state residents, regardless of the neighborhood in which they live. Complaint teams travel to smaller communities, hearing gripes and taking testimony regarding insurance practices—especially in ghetto areas where insurance problems are particularly difficult. The department requires all insurance companies doing business in Pennsylvania to appoint an ombudsman or similar complaint officer (the Commission itself appointed its own ombudsman). In 1971 the state also initiated the exposé of fraudulent mail-order insurance. This action, like many others generated by Denenberg, was soon copied by other commissioners across the nation.

In addition, a $10-million ambulance-chasing racket in Philadelphia was dutifully publicized. A model no-fault insurance law was developed, and a fact sheet on no-fault made available to the public. And policy readability guidelines, for the first time in regulatory history, have been drafted to help overcome vague and confusing language. Said Denenberg: "If we can put a man on the moon we ought to be able to write insurance policies the public can read."

A major new program was launched late in 1973 with three days of hearings on the safety of nuclear reactors and the adequacy of insurance protection for damage they might cause. This was the first comprehensive airing of the subject not controlled by the nuclear establishment.

Pennsylvania's Insurance Commission operates as an informal clearinghouse for interested consumer groups and government offices and stands ready to offer advice, provide technical assistance, and lend its support for reform activities. It retains the irreverent motto invoked by former commissioner Denenberg: "Populus Iamdudum Defutatus Est—The Consumer Has Been Screwed Long Enough."

The Prosecutor

The job of State's Attorney for Chittenden County, Vermont —whose 100,000 people comprise nearly a quarter of the state's total population—calls for long hours, a strong stomach, and a keen sense of humor. Patrick J. Leahy has them all.

Appointed to an unexpired term in May 1966, Leahy was the youngest man on record to be appointed a state's attorney in Vermont. Now his office has become one of the most important in the state government. It has maintained a better-than-90-per-cent conviction rate while trying the highest number of cases of any Vermont prosecutor. "We do not bring a case to trial," says Leahy, "unless we are convinced of the defendant's guilt, and we feel that we can win. To do otherwise is a waste of the taxpayers' money and the court's time."

Before Leahy took office, state's attorneys in Vermont were free to practice law on the side, and they all did. Leahy became more than a full-time prosecutor. One of his first moves was to throw away patronage. "The jobs on my staff go to the best qualified man or woman and they are strictly nonpartisan. The big problems in filling those jobs are not the qualifications, but finding men and women who will work seventy to eighty hours per week for low pay and be on call twenty-four hours a day." The public has returned him to office every two years since 1966, and by large electoral margins.

By taking positions which are sometimes controversial but always strong, Leahy has succeeded in challenging and updating the judicial system. Results to date: Chittenden

County obtained the first convictions in Vermont under the new water-pollution laws, the first "discharge permit" convictions, and the first conviction under Vermont's air-pollution statute. Hundreds of contacts were made during the time allowed to implement standards set down by new laws. Industries, individuals, junkyards, and dumps were approached and asked if they would make an honest effort to clean up before Leahy's office would be required to come back and prosecute them. The response was surprisingly effective. The state's attorney's hard line on pollution has reached into the most obscure places; the word is out to "clean up, watch your smoke and litter, or expect a visit from Leahy." Other state's attorneys in Vermont have followed Leahy's lead and have established similar tough enforcement of pollution laws.

Leahy has been cognizant of discrimination against women. He suggests that laws providing penalties for desertion and nonsupport should be modified "so that the issue to be resolved in each case hinges on which spouse is better able to provide support, rather than automatically place on the male the full responsibility." He also recommends "that the law be changed to cover situations where a male can be raped," and expresses "strong support for ratification of the Equal Rights Amendment by the Vermont Legislature." Leahy has taken assertive stances on the drug problem. He announced that his office will not seek prosecution of any marijuana cases (possession in Vermont is treated as a misdemeanor) except in the most extreme situations. At the same time, his staff has maintained the state's highest conviction rate against sellers of heroin and other hard drugs. Leahy's staff works with the University of Vermont, regional health agencies, and other groups to provide help for victims of drug abuse outside the criminal-justice system. Leahy further believes that the primary aim of drunken driving laws should be to get intoxicated drivers off the road, and proposes a realistic standard of what constitutes drunken driving: conviction or acquittal is determined on the basis of specific blood-alcohol levels.

In addition, the Chittenden Area Strike Force—an undercover operation (with the aid of personnel from the police departments, state police, and the governor's office) has been successful in removing several criminal gangs which operated, virtually unchecked, in the state for a decade. Leahy has also implemented a plan to institute a regional police force, combining the efforts and facilities of seven law-enforcement bodies in the county into one well-organized and quickly responsive agency.

For Leahy, a sense of humor is a sense of perspective. In 1971 he issued a memorandum to all police departments regarding public bathing:

> A number of law-enforcement agencies have asked this office for advice [on] the time-honored practice of unclothed swimming, known colloquially as "skinny-dipping." I was originally disinclined to slow the crime-fighting operation of the Chittenden County State's Attorney's Office to issue a memorandum of such minuscule moment. However, I have been reminded that in the past the plethora of paper from this office has included such legal landmarks as my position on the use of sparklers on the Fourth of July (a position hedged with great patriotic fervor) and the validity of upside-down license plates. . . . It appears that most Vermonters I've talked to have engaged in such scandalous activity at some time in their life. Times do change. Today such things are apparently allowable in most movies, on Canadian television, in the *National Geographic*, and *Life* magazine but by no means in the pristine streams and rivers of Vermont.

With this gently persuasive introduction he went on to propose reasonable guidelines for handling this problem.

Public demonstrations often require expert handling by a state's attorney. One Vermont encounter was cooled upon Leahy's arrival by his modulated explanation that students in the post office at the time had a "perfect right" to be in a public building, and that the authorities were "off base" in shutting down the elevators and confining the demonstrators to the lobby.

Leahy worked actively with the National District Attorneys' Association to obtain funds for instituting a full-time consumer fraud unit in his office. Theretofore, in Vermont as elsewhere, consumer fraud matters were handled solely by seeking refunds to the aggrieved party. Leahy anticipates that his office will now seek criminal prosecutions wherever possible. "It is my personal feeling," he says, "that many large concerns will continue to defraud consumers if they feel that they will only be required to make periodic restitutions to a percentage of those defrauded. On the other hand, if the officers of those corporations are brought into court to face criminal action and possible sentences, the fraudulent activity usually comes to a quick halt."

Patrick Leahy is far more interested in prosecuting for crimes against persons and property than for the so-called "victimless" crimes. "I can't see wasting money and time on 'thought control' prosecution—crimes like adultery, or homosexuality. These should be handled in other than a criminal way." He says that he simply does not have enough police to prosecute every crime on the books, and that if he must choose, he will go after the mugger and robber rather than the person who breaks into an isolated warehouse.

Leahy thinks of a society as being governed primarily by laws: if there is general disagreement with any particular law, it will be changed in a normal democratic fashion. The prosecutor is one of the single most powerful individuals in the American system of local government. He can refuse to bring charges as well as bring them. He is also in the position of being able to lead the public opinion in many areas of interpretation of the law. All told, Patrick Leahy's reasoned approach is exemplary.

The Bureaucrats: Watchdogs

In September 1968, the Comptroller General of the United States submitted a report to Congress on the "Need to Improve Regulatory Enforcement Procedures Involving Pesticides." The findings were based on a review by the General Accounting Office of the Department of Agriculture's law-enforcement activity during the mid-1960s. In particular, though, it was the exceptionally thorough work of two dedicated public servants—Morton Myers and Richard Chervenak—which proved that the Department's Pesticide Regulation Division had been shockingly incompetent in removing from the market hazardous or ineffective pesticides, many of which were being sold illegally.

The law itself is satisfactory. Since 1947 the Federal Insecticide, Fungicide, and Rodenticide Act has required that all pesticides shipped in interstate commerce be registered with the USDA. (The law is now administered by the Environmental Protection Agency.) To qualify for registration a pesticide must be proven both safe and effective when used as directed. The Act provides criminal penalties for the interstate shipment of pesticide products which are unregistered, adulterated, or "misbranded" (if labeling contains false or misleading statements or does not bear clearly understandable warnings). The USDA is authorized to initiate court proceedings for the seizure of dangerous or ineffective pesticides. Registration may be canceled at any time if the product or its labeling does not comply with the law, or if registration is not renewed every five years, or if the Secretary of Agriculture determines such action is necessary to prevent an imminent hazard to the public health. In addition, the Federal Food, Drug, and Cosmetic Act requires that a tolerance level for pesticide residues be established; food containing such residues is considered to be adulterated.

The primary responsibility for enforcing the law in this area had belonged to the PRD whose specialists were supposed to review data on products proposed for registration and determine their safety and efficacy, as well as the adequacy of label warnings and directions.

Myers and Chervenak exposed these key findings:

—Numerous pesticide products had been approved for registration over the objections of the Department of Health, Education, and Welfare as to their safety—in total disregard of statutorily required procedures.

—The PRD had approved products for uses which it knew or should have known were almost certain to result in illegal adulteration of food.

—The PRD failed to take adequate precautions to insure that pesticide product labels approved for registration clearly warn users against possible hazards, and had no procedures for cautioning users of potentially hazardous products.

—Information available to federal agencies concerning pesticide poisoning was inadequate and incomplete. The PRD made little effective use of even the limited data available.

—The PRD took neither prompt nor effective action to cancel a registered product it had reason to suspect as ineffective or potentially hazardous, and consistently failed to remove potentially hazardous products from marketing channels after their registrations had been suspended or canceled.

—The Agricultural Research Service failed to take appropriate precautions against appointment of consultants to positions in which their duties might conflict with the financial interests of their private employer.

Myers and Chervenak did not criticize the manner in which pesticides were collected and analyzed. What first raised their hackles was that, although fully 20 per cent of the 2751 samples reviewed by the PRD in fiscal 1966 were considered to be in major violation of the law, the division had neither procedures nor standards for obtaining information about the location of pesticide products, and it discovered that in general only the offending samples found at the inspected retail or wholesale outlet were removed. No attempt was made to determine whether additional quantities were in other markets.

Myers and Chervenak cited graphic failures by the PRD to remove dangerous and illegal products from store shelves. Registrations of fifty-nine products containing thallium were ordered canceled as of the end of August 1965—the result of a large number of reported poisonings. Despite such unequivocal action, the study disclosed that products containing thallium were found in six of twenty-two retail establishments visited in the Washington, D.C., area more than two years later.

Moreover, the PRD failed to take effective action in prosecuting those responsible for placing the illegal products on the market.

The two GAO researchers further charged that the PRD had no established procedures for determining the circumstances under which evidence of violations would be reported to the Department of Justice for prosecution. They found that, despite repeated violations by some shippers, not a single case was reported from 1955 through 1968.

Although the Insecticide, Fungicide, and Rodenticide Act requires that the Secretary of Agriculture give notice of all judgments entered, Myers and Chervenak found that from

1947 to November 1964 only eighteen public notices (summarizing the results of 515 judgments, primarily seizures) had been issued. They also discovered that no publications had come forth from November 1964 through December 1967, despite an accumulation during this period of about 250 judgments. The explanation offered for the USDA's failure was characteristically lame: the employee assigned to compiling the necessary information had retired and had not been replaced.

Even witnesses from the USDA acknowledged the report's findings, on both the lack of procedural machinery for prosecution and the total failure of the PRD's enforcement record. They further confirmed that no notices of judgment had been issued during a period of more than four years. Testimony at subcommittee hearings also cited the PRD's failure to remove illegal pesticide products from the market. A high official of the Agricultural Research Service admitted that, as of the end of 1966, PRD policy was to seize only the quantity of illegal pesticide products found at the location where the sample was taken, and that further, no efforts were made to locate additional quantities of illegal products or to order multiple seizures and remove them from distribution channels. It was also established that existing stocks of rat poison containing thallium had deliberately been left on the market after registrations for such use had been canceled due to reports of numerous injuries and deaths —particularly of children.

Largely as a result of efforts by a few dedicated public servants, such as Myers and Chervenak, acts of gross mismanagement and neglect by a key department of a federal agency are being brought to light. Their work, and the subsequent hearings by the House of Representatives Committee on Government Operations, uncovered malfeasance which could have ended in death for great numbers of unsuspecting adults and children.

The Bureaucrats:
Civil Rights' Enforcer

Bill Payne sits behind a large desk in a small yellow-tinted office at the end of a long, dreary hallway. His job: to help assure that federal civil-rights laws and regulations are carried out in the Department of Agriculture's Office of Equal Opportunity. The fact that his room is at the end of the hallway is accidental, he claims, but the symbolism is not lost on visitors familiar with the USDA's reputation on civil rights.

"Civil rights is the most significant social problem before the country today," says Payne. "It's like a bone that is caught in the throat. Unless it is removed, you will eventually starve to death. You can't get around it. You've got to deal with it."

Payne grew up in New Mexico, where his parents were school teachers, and he graduated from Baylor University in Texas. For a while he thought he wanted to go into the ministry, but soon learned—when a member of the church he was pastoring died—that he did not have enough experience to be able to understand human suffering. He joined the Air Force, but after getting married realized that he did not want a military career. He took up political science in graduate school, but ran out of money before completing his degree requirements. Then he applied for a federal job, and ended up at the United States Commission on Civil Rights.

"That was in the fall of 1964," Payne relates, "and there was a general mood of optimism with the passage of the Civil Rights Act in July. I was pretty naïve then, thinking that the civil-rights problems were licked. Little did I realize what has since become clear: our civil-rights problems were born out of generations of discrimination and neglect and at the rate we're going now, it will take generations to do away with them."

Most of his time at the Civil Rights Commission was spent on rural problems—examining agricultural programs to determine their impact on minority beneficiaries. It was from this experience that the emotional fervor with which he talks about the civil-rights problems of rural minority groups is derived. "I would literally cry when I looked at the figures on food programs and knew that they translated into human beings who were killing the family cat or eating the bark off trees. Fortunately the federal government has since responded to the food problem. It was, however, only a few years ago that only ten per cent of those in poverty were receiving food aid. Even today you look at some of the Indian reservations and some of the ghetto schools and you know we've got a long way to go."

Payne has never considered himself an activist. "Though I'm pretty good with ideas it has usually been up to someone else to carry them out." Several of his ideas, however, have contributed to major improvements in attacking poverty and civil-rights problems. He worked behind the scenes to help develop private studies that resulted in Congressional attention to national food programs. A 1970 article he wrote for the *Civil Rights Digest* helped focus national attention on the financial plight of predominantly black land-grant colleges, and resulted in legislation that enabled the USDA to increase its aid to those institutions from less than $400,000 in 1968 to $16 million in 1973. His research on discrimination in the State Cooperative Extension Services has engendered three law suits to bring relief in those southern states that still ran segregated systems. He is equally proud of suggesting the idea of a Federal Employee's Fast Day Committee, which organized a federal workers' one-day boycott of government cafeterias during the Poor Peoples Campaign and donated the money saved to that effort.

After almost eight years with the Civil Rights Commission, Payne moved to the USDA in the summer of 1972. There he is working to assure adequate representation of minority groups and women on agricultural advisory bodies, a procedure for enforcing nondiscrimination requirements in revenue-sharing programs, and a system whereby the civil-rights implications of policy actions will be weighed before decisions are made. The latter, he feels, is potentially one of the most important innovations in civil-rights enforcement techniques. "If we can get agreement that civil rights is an integral part of good program administration and institutionalize it as a part of decision-making, we will have gone a long way toward closing the gap in civil-rights enforcement by the federal government."

Payne is given to understatement when talking about himself. "I'm no hero," he says. "The real heroes are the people themselves. I'm just thankful I can play a part in the most significant social effort of our time—the civil-rights struggle for social justice. Martin Luther King said it all when he told us that we won't be free until everybody is free. I believe that and that's why I am where I am, doing what I am doing."

The Bureaucrats: Gadfly

The Code of Ethics for Government Service requires, in effect, that each civil servant act as an overseer of the public interest. Key provisions:

> Any person in Governmental service should: Put loyalty to the highest moral principles and to country above loyalty to persons, party, or government department. Uphold the Constitution, laws and legal regulations of the United States and of all governments therein and never be a party to their evasion. . . . Seek to find and employ more efficient and economical ways of getting tasks accomplished. . . . Expose corruption wherever discovered. Uphold these principles, ever conscious that public office is a public trust.

Unfortunately the Code remains little more than admonition, since Congress did not provide for penalties when one or more of its clauses is violated. Indeed, the system sometimes penalizes the government employee who takes such ethics to heart: whistle-blowing public servants are frequently disdained by colleagues. Disturbingly often they are silenced or intimidated. Civil-service regulations themselves help do the trick by tending to shield (and occasionally reward) incompetence and sloth, discouraging creativity and diligence, and undermining professional and individual responsibility.

Some civil servants nevertheless do nurture the whistle-blowing ethic within their agencies. At the Department of Housing and Urban Development, this is accomplished by way of an irreverent newsletter called *Impact*. "It's not sufficient to go into a bureaucracy on a one-shot deal, expose the inefficiency and mismanagement, write a report, get good press coverage, and then leave," says Al Ripskis, *Impact's* creator. "Unless a bureaucracy is constantly prodded and shaped from within, it has a tendency to slip back into its old ways."

Ripskis speaks as a self-appointed ombudsman for HUD. Since September 1972 he has been the guiding force behind *Impact*, which has dedicated itself to exposing waste, graft, mismanagement, corruption, incompetence, and discrimination. The subscription newsletter ($5 per year) is personal journalism of the Jack Anderson variety, but it is unique in government as a forum for open criticism of HUD in which its staff members are employed.

Ripskis had a predecessor at HUD, Jay Thal, whom he helped edit a similar newsletter called *Quest*. Thal was suddenly and suspiciously transferred by HUD to Alaska on a four-month assignment, a move that effectively put *Quest* out of business. But Ripskis soon founded *Impact*—and immediately put his own job on the line. "You can be sure they are going to be watching him very closely," *The Federal Times* (September 27, 1972) quoted one official—"not only HUD but the Civil Service Commission, and who knows, even some of the investigating arms of government."

Impact prints information fed surreptitiously to Ripskis by HUD staffers in Washington, as well as by HUD's regional offices. Among its choice scoops to date:

—A high official's cross-country junket with his female assistant-mistress, at taxpayers' expense, under the guise of an emergency fact-finding and rebuilding trip after hurricane Camille.

—Disclosure that HUD had spent $26,000 for two new 80-foot flag poles (besting the 75-foot poles of its neighbor, the Department of Transportation).

—Discovery that HUD has failed to comply with a

new law requiring submission of a report on the prevention of child poisoning by lead-based paint.

—Publication of a confidential memo from one of former Secretary George Romney's area directors, William Whitbeck of Detroit, containing severe criticism of Romney and his administration as Secretary of HUD.

Ripskis claims several hundred informants and contacts, and he is trying to organize an above-ground grapevine of like-minded HUD employees. Some forty assistants volunteer their time to produce and distribute the newsletter.

Debunking waste, production, and mismanagement in the bureaucracy is to Ripskis part of his job. He is quick to point out that his primary loyalty is to the taxpayer. To resign from the organization to which he takes such exception would be a cop-out. He implores colleagues to speak out. "How many times have we seen incompetence and waste? And what do we do? Do we look the other way? Do we shrug it off by thinking, Well, it won't do any good, so why rock the boat? or I have two kids to put through school, or I don't want to jeopardize my chances for promotion." Ripskis says that if he should be fired, "it won't stop my activities. I might even intensify them. I'd have more time."

Impact has already had a salutary effect in bringing about change—from Congress, from people within HUD who now feel less inhibited to express their ideas, and from the press. Problems and issues rarely examined by the public are now routinely being exposed through the newsletter. "*Impact* is hardly a professional job," wrote syndicated columnist Nicholas von Hoffman, "but it does give a rare look at the inside of a demoralized, leaderless, and corrupted department of government."

Ripskis and *Impact* suggest that other public servants with similar impulses should:

—Present the facts accurately and let them speak for themselves.

—Cultivate contacts with the media which can give intramural malfeasance national exposure, as well as publicize any retaliations or threats from higher-ups.

—Do all their whistle-blowing on their own time (Ripskis edits *Impact* only on evenings, weekends, and during lunch hours).

Although its journalistic outrage is somewhat lacking in editorial restraint and polish, *Impact*'s concerns are specific, well documented, and genuine. A recent issue charged that new HUD Secretary James T. Lynn, by requisitioning additional parking spaces for his staff, deprived certain handicapped employees of easy access to their offices. Another article lashed out at HUD's severe procrastination (at that point eighteen months past the announced deadline) in reporting to Congress its recommendations for legislation on lead paint:

> We've been told that an emasculated draft of this report is being bounced around from one HUD office to another.
> The additional month's delay means 17 more children dead, 67 with irreversible brain damage, 267 with moderate to severe brain damage, and 1,333 kids requiring treatment for some other lead paint-induced ailment. . . .
> The cumulative casualty count due to HUD's tardiness is as follows:
> 302 children dead
> 1,207 with irreversible brain damage
> 4,626 moderate to severe brain damage
> 23,994 requiring treatment of some kind
> How many more, Mr. Lynn?

The same issue carried an interview with Lynn, who succeeded Romney in February 1973 as Secretary of HUD.

Apparently Ripskis will not be sent the way of his predecessor Thal.

> LYNN: My basic problem has been getting the top team on board so that we could put these systems into effect. It seems to me it does no good to try to put these into effect where you have people who are transitional running the shops. I've got to make it clear to the people who are Assistant Secretaries of what I expect from them. So that they know they have the responsibility to put those into effect down the line. I have found that when you deal with people who are only transitional, all you do is lose time. I'd rather do it right and wait a little bit to do it.
>
> RIPSKIS: Well, thank you very much, Mr. Secretary. I really appreciate having this opportunity to speak with you.
>
> LYNN: And I appreciate it, too, and I look upon you as a kind of ombudsman for me. No, I mean that. You get more and you will hear more where you are than I get any day of the week. Because there are all kinds of insulation techniques. Nobody wants to give me the bad news in that regard. They all want to look good—that's great, that's human nature, everybody does. But to the extent you hear this kind of stuff, if you see something going on down there, I want to know it.

People Acting Together

*America is not anything if it consists of
each of us. It is something only if it consists
of all of us; and it can consist of all of us
only as our spirits are banded together
in a common enterprise.*
—Woodrow Wilson

In Groups

The Television Monitors

Times have changed from the days before television, when children's entertainment was largely self-generated. Even preschool children (ages three to five) watch an average of twenty-two to twenty-five hours of television every week—a daily activity second only to sleep in time consumed. Television has become, for many families, the young child's surrogate parents.

What does the tube teach? A recent study finds the Saturday-morning video playpen stuffed with a wonderland of not-so-juvenile junk:

—Over half of all program time is devoted to crime, the supernatural, or strife between characters. Seventy-one per cent of the stories include at least one episode of human violence, less than 3 per cent is devoted to family life, religion, business, government, literature, or the arts.

—Cartoons and other animated shows account for two thirds of available viewing.

—A commercial is shown an average of every two minutes. (This is a far higher average than that for adult programs.) It is often difficult even for grownups to figure out where the cartoons end and the huckstering begins.

Action for Children's Television, a national organization of parents and professionals with members in every state, is seeing to it that the world's most powerful communication medium is used more effectively and creatively. In business to bring about a change in the decision-making process for children's programing, the ACT works to make television's true impact known to those who may have dismissed its current significance or ignored its potential to enrich young minds and personalities. The group's approach is positive. It pressures both broadcasters and advertisers to provide programing of the highest possible quality for children of different ages, to eliminate commercialism, and to explore new systems of financial support including underwriting and public service funding.

The ACT was formed in 1968 by four women from Newton Centre, Massachusetts (Evelyn Sarson, Peggy Charren, Judith Chalfen, and Lillian Ambrosino), all of whom had watched the kiddy shows and come away with 1) headaches and 2) the conclusion that most programs were little more than attention-getters for the hard sell. Many programs seemed even to ignore the attention-getting phase.

From close interrogation of broadcasters, network executives, advertisers, performers, and producers, the ACT decided that the people who plan network children's programing know little about their audience, and often do not care to learn. The group concluded that improved programing, free of commercials, would come only from direct citizen pressure upon the regulators and the national networks.

The ACT petitioned the Federal Communications Commission in February 1970 to eliminate commercials and gratuitous product plugs from all children's programing. It suggested that fourteen hours per week of commercial-free kids' shows be required as part of each station's public-service obligation. To everyone's surprise, the FCC published the ACT guidelines almost verbatim as a Public Notice, inviting all interested parties (read "broadcasters") to submit comments. Action for Children's Television quickly mobilized a letter-writing campaign; by July 1971 the FCC had heard from over 60,000 people, most of whom supported the Public Notice. By 1973 there were over 100,000 replies from individuals, groups, and organizations representing millions of concerned citizens.

Since the FCC rarely intervenes in questions of program content, its move in this instance was significant. The Public Notice had no legal force, but it gave warning to broadcasters that the government would not stand idly by. Although reluctant at first, the industry finally responded to stiff prodding by the ACT and the FCC (and to the success of nonviolent, noncommercial programs like *Sesame Street*) with a small measure of responsible (though not advertisement-free) children's programs.

While it is concerned about the violence on television, the ACT concentrates its efforts on the way television hustles kids. "As long as selling remains a primary function of children's TV," says Ms. Charren, "the programs will continue to try to hold a child's attention by the surest means possible. The sad fact is that violence is one of the best attention grabbers."

Thus, the ACT went to the Federal Trade Commission in November 1971, petitioning for elimination of all vitamin advertisements from children's television. In response to the ACT's pressure, by the fall of 1972 the three vitamin companies advertising on children's programs had switched to adult television. The ACT has returned to the FTC three more times to demand similar bans on toy, food, and sugar product ads. The FTC's right to issue the trade-regulation rules request by the ACT was being contested in the courts and has only recently regained the power to do so. The ACT now awaits the FTC's response.

The ACT also encourages self-regulation. Local stations generally subscribe to the Codes of the National Association of Broadcasters. ACT monitors compare the various guidelines with what they see actually televised, and report instances of deviation to the networks, the local broadcast-

ers' association and the FCC. The group is seldom satisfied
with form-letter reassurances: if the offensive programs continue to run and no action is taken, they demand good
answers as to why. The ACT publishes a newsletter which
has a national distribution of over 20,000.

The continuing battle to make children's television responsive to social needs must be fought from a broader base,
but the ACT makes the following suggestions to parents:

—Set acceptable rules (consulting with the children)
about television-watching, such as specified time on school
days.

—Pay attention to program content, and note the alternative choices offered by public television.

—Let the appropriate people or organizations know
what upsets you and what pleases you about children's
television. Write to the station, the advertisers, and the
networks. (Since the stations are licensed for three years
by the FCC and are supposed to meet the "interests, convenience, and necessity of the community they serve,"
broadcasters are sensitive to criticism.")

Problems of television advertising and children are particularly suited to citizen action. It requires neither expensive
technical expertise for an individual nor an *ad hoc* group
to get started—actually little more than a television set and
materials for letter-writing.

By its efforts the ACT hopes to increase adult involvement
in what children watch and to contribute to an era of excellence in television. Until that day dawns, the group offers
disgruntled parents a sure-fire remedy when all else fails to
yield responsible programing: it suggests that they simply
turn off the set.

The Government Watchers

Not all Americans are willing to stand idly by thinking their government is its own best watchdog, hoping for integrity without actively demanding it.

The Citizens Action Program of Chicago, with chapters throughout the city's metropolitan area, has been shaking waste, graft, and corruption out of local government for the past three years. "And our members and leaders," says vice president Paul Booth," are drawn from that segment of society that has been dubbed the Silent Majority." The group's first target, back in 1970, was pollution. Attention was focused on property tax structures when it was discovered that industrial polluters were also cheating the city's taxpayers of millions of dollars each year. Now there are coalitions fighting neighborhood deterioration and high-rise construction on the lakeshore. They have also managed to defeat a proposed Crosstown Expressway—a twenty-mile, billion-dollar project that would have displaced 10,400 people and destroyed scores of demonstrably healthy communities.

In its war on corporate tax cheaters, as in its other battles, the CAP's main weapons have been accumulation of accurate facts and direct action. Data are dug out of obscure places like assessment rolls. A research staff investigates issues that are of concern to all Chicagoans. The group's published studies of assessment procedures, mass-transit alternatives to urban expressways, and property tax classification have gained national attention. Accurate, detailed, and comprehensive information helps the citizens effectively confront corporate and political powers-that-be.

The CAP has improved the quality of Chicago air by forcing Commonwealth Edison, the Metropolitan Sanitary District, and U.S. Steel to adopt and implement pollution-control systems. It has helped save Lake Michigan as a water resource and recreational area by successfully opposing a projected billion-dollar airport on Lake Michigan. It has saved 5 per cent on the citizens' property tax bills by forcing reassessment of five race tracks, four steel mills, and several downtown Loop office buildings that had been given tax breaks by the county assessor. (Underassessment of the four steel mills cost Cook County taxpayers around $27 million in 1970 and over $100 million over the last ten years.) In addition, the Illinois Central Railroad was caught taking an exemption to which it was not entitled. Still another study disclosed that the Cook County property-tax-collection process was rigged to make the county borrow to meet current expenses. As a result, county taxpayers had shelled out about $37.5 million in interest payments in 1970 to wealthy bankers and investors—and over $109 million between 1966 and 1970.

When the citizens group learned that the Chicago School Board had been leasing property to the First Federal Savings and Loan—for $73,000 per year, though it was worth at least $320,000—members opened accounts to become shareowners in time for the annual meeting, at which they raised the issue from the floor. Through their efforts the amount of property tax rebates to senior citizens and the disabled was doubled, and a tax rollback was forced in South Shore and Beverly, where homeowners had previously been over-assessed by an average of 30 per cent.

For the CAP, research is only the first step in applying public pressure where it has the most effect—on the people in power. The cutting edge of the group's work is the organized and disciplined activity of its thousands of members. These members, recruited for active participation by other activist-members, commit themselves to support of particular issues. Mass action has gained quick access to records of the county assessor, the school board, and the Crosstown Expressway planners. Though the citizens know that for all their local victories the power of corporations and private wealth remains secure, they nevertheless persist in their desire to be part of a national assault on that power.

Projects in progress include:

—Extending the battle against unfair tax guidelines and assessing practices (the battle is on two fronts: for statewide property tax relief for small homeowners and renters, and for an assessment system that relieves the burden on overassessed homeowners and small businesses, and closes loopholes that benefit corporations and private developers.

—Preventing a high-rise glut on the lakefront (program affiliates—the Sheridan Highrise Opposition and the Gordon Terrace Organization on the North Side— are challenging the right of land speculators to exploit Chicago neighborhoods through unrestricted high-rise development. Using carefully planned pressure on public officials, the groups are leading a coalition of citizen forces in the fight for controlled density zoning on the lakefront and expanded park land).

—Mobilizing senior citizens for justice (the Senior Citizens Clubs affiliated with the CAP have achieved a twenty-four-hour, seven-day-week transit fare, and are campaigning to make all necessities such as phone service and prescription drugs available to all senior citizens at prices that all can afford).

—Organizing citizen pressure against irresponsible banks to stop "red-lining" (a practice that denies mortgage and home-improvement financing to older neighborhoods while funneling the community's savings deposits into speculative developments in far distant suburbs).

—Organizing to reverse the present trend toward sky-rocketing food prices by concerted consumer action.

The victories it has won on behalf of the environment and the taxpayer have made it possible for the CAP to raise 90 per cent of its $75,000 yearly budget by door-to-door solicitation of homeowners and merchants. Successes to date appear impressive, and they are. But their main importance is what they promise. The Chicago group's efforts, and those of other citizens' organizations like it, have just begun.

The Rehabilitators

In the spring of 1971 two independent Congressional investigations confirmed rumors that as many as 15 per cent of all American soldiers in Vietnam had become addicted to heroin.

The news of course caused an immediate sensation, not just because of the facts themselves but what they reflected about the war and the nation. The 15 per cent figure could not be shrugged off as a momentary aberration or a series of isolated incidents; quite the contrary, it suggested a deep and pervasive alienation among the American fighting men—a collapse of discipline and a breakdown of morale. Those who had not been permitted to come home were seeking their own kind of unilateral withdrawal.

Until recently the soldier on drugs was treated as a criminal, and whatever problems he had were deemed his own fault. The Army's first and only concern was the degree to which he represented a threat to its mission, and its primary response was either imprisonment or discharge. But neither punishment of individuals nor threats of more universal discipline inhibited the proliferating tide of addiction. Even as heroin use assumed epidemic proportions in 1970, the military publicly denied the extent of the problem. The traditional policy—prosecution and punitive discharge —had been acceptable when the number involved was small, but the prospect of legions of untreated heroin addicts returning from Vietnam was causing general alarm. By the next spring, with the Congressional investigations and the public's subsequent clamor all but impossible to ignore, the disclaimers ended. The military was forced to accept responsibility for its drug problem and embark on a serious program of rehabilitation.

The Navy and Air Force chose to set up centralized treatment facilities, while the Army followed a decentralized approach to permit more flexibility and experimentation. The Veterans Administration, likewise pushed into the area of drug abuse and rehabilitation, opened five drug-treatment centers in January 1971. But no matter what the form of rehabilitation, universal problems persisted. One has been the disjunction between the military's primary goal—to return men to duty—and the desires of the patients, which are usually the reverse. There is also a contradiction between the ethics of therapy, requiring confidentiality between doctor and patient, and the military imperative that every commander know the physical and psychological condition of his men. Complicating the ambiguity of treatment even further, most soldier-patients tend to resist the notion that they are sick. In general the early growth of the active military's programs was chaotic and showed much too little planning. And the returning veterans did not fit into the hospitals, their life-styles running counter to that of the wards in which they were placed.

Probably the most remarkable drug program for Vietnam veterans was a completely independent operation called the Drug Mending Zone. Created by a group of veterans already active in a community-wide drug rehabilitation program named Services for Education and Rehabilitation in Addiction (SERA), the DMZ was the result of many hours of research comparing the neighborhood addict with the veteran. The group's conclusion: the two kinds of addicts must be treated differently.

The DMZ existed for several years in a decaying South Bronx tenement, where it made known its intentions with a characteristically enthusiastic announcement: "Operation Clean-Up is now under way. Under cover of South Bronx air pollution, seventeen (17) veterans attacked and secured the fifth floor of 1027 E. 167th Street at 1425 hours on 8-17-71. We have now established a foothold (which at present is reminiscent of a foxhole) and the enemy, shocked and humiliated, is retreating rapidly. The entire building should be within our grasp in no time."

Within months the DMZ had attracted more than eighty Vietnam veterans with drug problems (several times as many as any of the drug-free VA programs). Choosing against putting the man through traditional drug treatment, the DMZ instead harnessed their energies into rebuilding and reclaiming part of the desolate South Bronx slum where they lived.

Flags outside identified headquarters as a veterans' center and a drug-free community: within—a bustle of activity. The DMZ emphasized remedial education and training in useful skills. Experienced teachers were brought in to conduct classes and seminars. Although discipline was strict, the residents were by no means insulated from the community: the DMZ ran special programs for young children in the neighborhood and was instrumental in negotiating a truce between local gangs. During its brief existence, the DMZ successfully treated over 350 veterans.

The contrast between the DMZ and the VA's drug programs could not have been more striking. At the VA hospitals patients idle their time away watching television, playing pool, or otherwise lolling aimlessly. Treatment takes place only during certain hours of the day; the rest of the time is vacant. At the DMZ the atmosphere was electric. There was none of the lethargy and boredom one senses at VA facilities, probably because the DMZ provided the opportunity for constructive expression—not through makework, arts and crafts or occupational therapy, but by organizing patients into a corps of active community volunteers.

An especially dramatic contrast was reflected in the rela-

tionship between staff personnel and members. At the DMZ
everyone was a former addict, a product of the same harsh
wartime environment—this in contrast to VA hospitals,
where a mostly professional staff handles patients with clin-
ical detachment. Among VA staff the will may be there
but the spirit is lacking.

The bitterness of the veterans toward the military remains
intense. SERA chieftain Frank Gracia says that once a
veteran is free of drugs the real task begins: "Institutional
detoxification to get the military out of their systems."
Although the DMZ went a long way toward accomplishing
both, it was forced to close its doors when the necessary
funding could no longer be found to support its rehabilitation efforts.

The Highway Fighters

When in 1957 the District of Columbia Highway Department submitted a comprehensive highway plan for the Capital area—still today the master blueprint for Washington—few people took notice. But, by 1965, citizens in various neighborhoods had become alarmed that an interstate freeway would cut directly through their communities, thousands of families would be displaced, park land would be lost, air and noise pollution would proliferate.

Shortly thereafter, local associations banded together to form the "Metropolitan Citizens' Committee for Rapid Transit," which became the Emergency Committee on the Transportation Crisis. Over the past ten years the ECTC has strikingly illustrated what can be done by a loosely organized citizen coalition against the entrenched powers of the highway lobby.

Located in Washington, D.C., a city which has been virtually blackmailed into runaway expansion of the freeway, the ECTC created the organization and led the struggle against unlimited construction of unneeded and destructive highways. The group developed as a loose and freewheeling organization, without dues or membership, and with no formal structure or line of command. From the first, anyone who opposed freeways could consider himself a member of the ECTC. Initiative is taken as the need arises, functions are assumed by those best qualified to perform at any given moment. There are no bylaws. Informality, cemented by nothing more than a common cause, has been a major reason for the ECTC's success in a city with a unique governmental arrangement by which the only elected officials are, even now, a sole nonvoting delegate to Congress and members of the school board.

The ECTC quickly adopted one key policy: no more of the traditional piecemeal opposition by particular neighborhoods, but a unified effort to achieve "not another inch of freeway." Members reasoned that since all segments of the area's highway network were to be connected, construction of any *single* segment would increase pressure to build on others; they also correctly assumed that opposition to all sections of the freeway system would bring support from all sections of the city. Indeed, the residents of Georgetown, mostly white, upper-level income, and residents of Brookland, mostly black, lower and middle income, protested arm in arm at freeway construction sites. This hard-nosed and uncompromising stand startled Washington highway officials.

The ECTC's meetings are attended by an extraordinary diversity of people—black and white, rich and poor, suburban and inner-city residents, religious leaders and political activists. Members make efforts to disseminate information regarding freeways to all social sectors in the city. The most important policy is the commitment to action. The Committee deems it essential that large groups attend all government highway hearings. Such "bird-dogging" of issues prevents *fait accompli* rebuttals.

Highlights reflecting the extent to which the ECTC is seen and heard are:

—*March 1966:* ECTC forced release of a report by Arthur D. Little, Inc., which had been commissioned by the D.C. Highway Department. (The Study found that the planning process in the Washington, D.C. area had been totally inadequate and recommended no further freeway construction in the District. It was subsequently rejected by the D.C. government and withdrawn from public use.)

—*November 1966:* A lawsuit was filed against the Highway Department, based on procedural illegalities in the planning process. Lawyers were supplied at a reduced fee from a large law firm in the District. The case was first decided in favor of the highway officials, but the Court of Appeals reversed in the citizens' favor. All roads named in the suit were termed illegal. (A precedent was also set that interstate highway officials must still obey local statutes as well as those in the Federal Aid Highway Act, setting forth requirements for interstate projects. The courts can thus stop freeway construction until all planning laws and requirements are met.)

—*June 1968:* A National Coalition on the Transportation Crisis opened channels of communication among citizen groups from different cities. (Other such conferences have been held since.)

—*December 1968:* The National Capital Planning Commission and the City Council ratified a modified regional comprehensive plan, in response to lobbying and pressure brought by ECTC members, so as to delete freeways. (The plan called for "no new 'gateways' to the city," effectively doing away with the proposed Three Sisters Bridge and North Central Freeway.)

—*January 1969:* The Mayor of Washington was persuaded to intervene in the Highway Department's illegal demolition of private homes along proposed (and still disputed) freeway routes. (The Mayor's action came after some twenty meetings between D.C. officials and the ECTC, which included rallies that resulted in several arrests.)

—*October 1969:* The ECTC organized a large demonstration at the site of the proposed Three Sisters Bridge to protest any additional freeway construction—because highway officials had continued to let contracts for bridge construction, and Congress, by threatening to withhold subway construction money, had pressured the D.C. City Council into reversing its position against the bridge.

—*January 1970 on:* A bus boycott was organized to dramatize the inadequacies of the Washington, D.C. public transportation system. (ECTC members drove cars and borrowed privately owned buses to help get people to work during the boycott.)

The ECTC disavows violence, but realizes that quiet meetings, an organizational bureaucracy, and letter writing—when not backed up by action—are not very productive. So the following tactical points are stressed:

—Keep basic issues simple—don't allow legal complexities to obscure the important issues.

—Politicize every issue—what happens depends directly upon politics and usually has very little to do with technical points. Always attempt to expose the *motivations* of highway-oriented politicians. What connections do politicians have with highway interests?

—Watch carefully for violations of laws and regulations —do the careful research necessary for public ombudsmanship.

—Stand strongly on principle (as opposed to engaging in "deals" and "trade-offs").

—Make effective use of slogans ("Not One More Inch of Freeway," "White Men's Roads Thru Black Men's Homes").

The ECTC emphasizes the principles upon which the United States Constitution is based—the equal worth of all people and the right of citizens to influence decisions of their government. Sums up one member: "If you truly believe in social justice and the democratic process—then you do what you can to achieve it. There is no reason to operate in any other way. We are simply exercising the full range of our constitutional rights."

The Road Users

Many motor-club managements are part of the highway lobby, a vast informal network of roadbuilders, automobile manufacturers, and related industries whose managers and directors frequently interlock through club directorships. As a result a large number of clubs often seem more interested in selling auto insurance and travel packages than in pushing for safer cars, lower repair costs, and better service.

Most members of the Automobile Association of America are unaware that their local club affiliates can do much more than provide maps and an occasional tow or emergency road service. A notable exception is the constituency of the Auto Club of Missouri, which makes well known its firm policy positions and reform programs in the areas of automobile and highway safety, air pollution, mass transportation, and car insurance. Missouri Auto Club President H. Sam Priest maintains that as a matter of simple obligation an auto club ought to advertise that they do more than provide the traditional road services. A great many Missourians seem to get the message: some 370,000 are members—making it the nation's fifth largest automobile club. (There are also members in thirty counties of Illinois and two of Kansas.) Although the Missouri club has in many instances supported new road construction, it does not automatically endorse the assumption that more automobiles and freeways are necessary or beneficial, and it hasn't hesitated to look critically at the products from Detroit—some of which it has attacked as "overpowered, fragile, and dangerous."

The Auto Club of Missouri does not shy away from

potential or real controversy. Because one of its officers was worried about the carbon-monoxide levels in the passenger compartments of Corvairs, the club obtained the necessary testing equipment and undertook a special study, which it completed and turned over to a Senate Committee some six months before the National Highway Traffic Safety Administration issued its warning about the Corvair's exhaust fumes. After the NHTSA published a consumer-protection bulletin calling attention to engine-mount failures in General Motors cars, especially 1965–69 Chevrolets, the Missouri Club decided to examine all brands. It had always checked mounts as a routine part of its main-line inspection, but in rechecking accumulated data on 536 previously examined vehicles it found failures and defects on all makes and models, not merely on GM products. (There were engine-mount failures on 29 per cent of the GM cars, 22 per cent of the Fords, 10 per cent of the Chryslers, and 5 per cent of American Motors automobiles.) Broken mounts were found in 1970 and 1971 models as well as in cars that had been built in prior years.

The Auto Club of Missouri continually seeks new ways to expand services to members and give them accurate information about automobiles and highways. Thus it has initiated a number of unusual consumer-oriented programs, among them a diagnostic car clinic, where a member can have 500 items checked for $17.50. A computerized data bank collects information on all defects found by the clinic, and provides it to federal agencies, manufacturers, and others concerned with automobile safety. Priest was first attracted to the idea of a diagnostic clinic after having visited similar operations in Belgium and Austria. That was in 1966. Within a year Missouri's $350,000 facility, the largest of its kind in the United States, was constructed. But its uniqueness is its independence, not its size. Offering a complete inspection at such low cost, for the past two years the clinic has operated on a break-even basis—with annual expenses offset by inspection revenue.

The Auto Club of Missouri also operates a series of two-day "Ladies Car Seminars" and a bicycle-skill training program to encourage safe vehicle operation through all types of traffic and road conditions. Through its membership publication (*The Midwest Motorist*) it offers constructively energetic criticism of Missouri's mandatory inspection law, in addition to disseminating information about the club's various programs (which are initiated and carried out by management and staff in line with policies determined by a board of governors and its executive committee). A newsletter, *The Automobile and Our Lives*, is sent to about 3500 traffic and police officials, news editors, municipal judges, and state and federal representatives.

Says Priest: "The Auto Club's main purpose is to help its members and the public get the safest, most economical, most convenient, and most pleasurable use of their motor cars."

The Land Bankers

Even in white communities, the number of middle-income land owners is on the decline—largely because of the increasing agglomeration of thousands of family farms into large-scale business operations. Land not under corporate control is frequently bought up by private speculators. The government's own "agricultural stabilization" programs have been instrumental in the regrouping of real estate.

Despite notable improvements in the racial climate during the past decade, the rural South continues to appear largely inhospitable to many social changes that might strike a more equitable balance in the political and economic power held by whites and blacks. In 1950, more than 12 million acres of land in the South was owned in full or in part by black people. By 1964, however, the figure had dropped to some 7.2 million acres, a startling decrease of some 40 per cent; the preliminary returns from the 1970 agricultural census suggest that the decline in black land-ownership continues unabated (down to 6 million acres in 1974). In a sense this trend prefigures the black community's lessening stake in America, at the same time that it is winning major battles, in the courts and elsewhere, for "equality."

To solve the problem for blacks, a group of concerned individuals in 1970 solicited contributions to support a "Land Bank" through an advertisement in *The New York Times*. Response to the ad was disappointing, but the group, undaunted, proposed the establishment of The Emergency Land Fund, and the idea slowly caught on with support from foundations and private contributors. By June 1972, a board of directors had been formed and staff hired. Now, fortified with two years' research into the patterns and causes of diminished black land ownership (and into black attitudes toward the problem), The Emergency Land Fund is in operation in seven southern states: Virginia, North Carolina, Georgia, Alabama, Mississippi, and Louisiana.

The Fund's initial program concerns itself with land retention—helping blacks hold the realty they already own. One of the reasons people lose their land is its unprofitability, so the Fund devotes some of its resources to technical assistance and land development. (The general policy is to cooperate with existing agencies for such services where they are available.) Land acquisition is considered where circumstances warrant; in such cases title to land may be vested in the hands of poor people, or they may be granted long-term leases on land which they wish actively to use.

The Fund has identified three leading causes for involuntary loss of land: tax sales, partitions, and foreclosures. Although none are in themselves illegal, investigations have revealed that a great deal of chicanery bordering on the illegal is regularly practiced by unscrupulous whites against unsuspecting and unsophisticated Southern blacks. In addition, various state laws permit ownership by adverse possession, transference of title to third parties who voluntarily pay the taxes on the land of others, partition of heirs' properties without regard to the nature of the petitioners' degree of interest, foreclosure proceedings on real property without consideration of the size of debt or the status of the debtor —all of these often work to the great disadvantage of the black community.

Such practices are attacked in a variety of ways. Successful projects with regard to tax sales have already been run in South Carolina and Mississippi. The method is to scan the legal notices of pending tax sales, to identify the blacks whose land is being sold, and to make sure they are notified. Once alerted to the danger of losing their land, most of the persons reached either pay the taxes themselves or ask the Fund for assistance.

A mechanism has also been devised to thwart partition sales, frequently used as a means for selling the land out from under a land-poor family that depends on the property for its shelter and sustenance. The Fund has earmarked a portion of its money to enter fair market-price bids at such auctions. Blacks are encouraged to write wills that prevent easy exploitation. In some cases the foreclosure sale is fully justified because of the willful neglect of the landowner. Ferreting out foreclosures that merit assistance is difficult. Low-interest loans are made available to prevent foreclosure where appropriate; in some cases steps are taken to correct the situation which precipitated the foreclosure—often the misuse or nonuse of the property. In such situations, after taking steps to insure that the immediate crisis is resolved, the Fund refers the landowner to agencies with programs to help inefficient farmers achieve higher yields from their land. Additional capital or technical assistance and cooperative relationships with other farmers are arranged. Consolidation of very small plots and the establishment of a land trust or experimental types of communities are other techniques for helping rural people remain on the land. The Fund's legal staff has prepared a simple booklet of Do's and Dont's for poor black landowners. The second level of preventive action will be the provision of legal advice to poor black landowners who are encountering problems with respect to retaining their land.

The disappearance of the modest-size black landholder means a decline of black holdings generally, given the paucity of wealthy blacks and the virtual absence of a black corporate sector. In an economy where agriculture contributes

less and less to the national income and to the level of employment, the economic significance of the decline in black land
ownership is hardly noticed. Its social and political significance, however, may be explosive.

The Health Protectors

"Health care is a right, not a privilege." That is the sometimes strident motto of a growing number of citizens, both within and outside the medical profession, who have taken it upon themselves to create a viable alternative to traditional systems of health-care delivery.

Since the Haight-Ashbury Free Clinic opened its doors in San Francisco seven years ago, similar ventures have sprouted all over the country. Haight-Ashbury was spawned as a freewheeling response to the drug casualties that resulted when hundreds of young people flocked into the Bay Area in 1967 for a summer of love, freedom, and mind expansion; the clinic's hassle-free, no-questions-asked atmosphere also helped it treat people with venereal disease and minor injuries. The need was not limited to San Francisco. Upward of 380 free clinics have opened from coast to coast, seeing tens of thousands of patients annually, and staffed by many hundreds of community activists and volunteer health workers.

The free clinic movement has an organization, the National Free Clinic Council, which was formed in 1968 largely through the efforts of David Smith, medical director of the Haight-Ashbury center. All clinics providing free primary health-care services automatically become members of the Council, which hopes to gain access to health-care funding available at the national level, and to distribute money equally to its members.

All the clinics share to one degree or another the twin conviction that the American medical system does not meet the people's needs and that it must be radically restructured. The principles on which they operate:

—Health care is a right and should be free at the point of delivery.

—Services should be comprehensive, unfragmented, and decentralized.

—Medicine should be demystified—health care should be rendered courteously and educationally, and patients, when possible, should be permitted to choose among alternative methods of treatment.

—Health-care institutions should be governed by the people who use and work in them.

"There is a large group of people in America who are medically disenfranchised," says Camille Heard, a spokeswoman for the National Free Clinic Council. "They either can't or won't receive necessary health care. There are no family doctors left in the inner cities. They have moved out to the suburbs where the money is. The few big city hospitals that do have clinics are a major hassle. You have to tell them how much your grandmother made when she was thirteen years old to become eligible for membership, and then you have to wait for a different doctor each time. Money is probably one of the biggest barriers. We did a survey in the Ashbury community last year and that was mentioned about sixty-five per cent of the time by the respondents as the reason they do not get the particular kind of health care they needed. For other people it's a language or cultural barrier. They may speak only Spanish and when they go there they can't tell the doctor where it hurts. Or they are black, and the doctor isn't even too certain he wants to touch a black person. Or they have long hair and the nurse in the reception area says, 'Have you had a bath lately?' There are a lot of cultural hassles."

Most free clinics provide the kind of services one might find in a neighborhood first-aid station—if such things existed. Their function rarely extends beyond routine stop-gap care and screening, pregnancy and VD testing, and treatment of colds, abrasions, and infections. They all see an urgent need to do more preventive work, but free clinics are forced to rely on more limited resources than any other medical institution. Most have decided that it is better to turn people away or limit the scope of their services rather than sacrifice the quality of services they are able to provide. Nevertheless, there are some clinics which offer a number of paramedical programs, as well as things like legal and housing advice, clothing exchanges, and surplus food pantries. Nearly all have various kinds of counseling services—drug, abortion, group—and some are able to sponsor dental care.

At first glance it would appear there are many variations on the free-clinic theme: they may be founded by medical practitioners seeking alternative forms of practice, by political parties to develop a particular constituency, or by neighborhood groups interested in providing a necessary local service. They can serve social dropouts, college communities, working classes, ghetto areas, or an all-female population. But they also share a number of common characteristics. Ethnic and cultural diversity is most prominent; depending on the area, there are large numbers of black, Chicano, Latino, native American, and migrant patients. Usually, free clinics are located near a main thoroughfare (like Telegraph Avenue in Berkeley, Greenmount Avenue in Baltimore, Wisconsin Avenue in Washington, D.C.) and are housed in renovated quarters. The Washington Free Clinic uses space donated by a church in Georgetown; the Baltimore operation rents a building located in the ghetto between The Johns Hopkins University and Memorial Stadium. The atmosphere is decidedly informal and unclinical. A reception area greets visitors with second-hand furniture, a donation box, and reading matter—ranging from underground newspapers to specially prepared guides on communicable diseases and nutrition. Examining rooms are often divided by wood partitions or curtains, separate from a modest lab and pharmacy.

In most free clinics almost everything is donated: rooms constructed and decorated by volunteer labor, medical equipment contributed by doctors' widows or hospitals moving to new facilities, drugs given by drug companies. Perhaps the most vulnerable characteristic of free clinics is that they must rely on medical personnel to volunteer their services. While doctors may pick and choose from among the clinics where they'd like to be, the clinics cannot afford to ask even an unpopular physician to go elsewhere.

The turnover is greater among the other volunteer help, which may include nurses, coordinator-receptionists, people's counselors and therapists, laboratory technicians, and patient advocates. Indeed, the bulk of the labor contributed to free clinics comes from nonprofessionals, most of whom have had no formal health-science education. Patients are encouraged to join in with the paper work. Nearly all clinics put a good deal of emphasis on the transfer of skills, creating a pool of paramedical workers and helping to demystify the practice of medicine. Doctors can often not be distinguished from patients or nonmedical volunteers.

The role of the patient advocate is an important one in most free clinics. He serves to help the patient understand medical procedures, assure follow-up treatment or referral when necessary, and protect against therapeutic or psychic abuses. The advocate takes the patient's history, discusses his complaint, tells him what the clinic can do to help, and what it cannot do. He is also responsible for insuring that the patient understands the doctor's recommendations and gets prescriptions filled.

Free clinics have their shortcomings. According to a bulletin put out by the Health Policy Advisory Center, they "are not successful in eliminating some of the principal disadvantages of out-patient departments: waiting time is long, there are no appointments, follow-up is shoddy, continuity of care is almost impossible."

But as Camille Heard points out: "Free clinics represent an alternative for those medically disenfranchised people. They don't impose the kind of sterile environment which hospitals have that turn most people off. I think the 'free' in free clinics also means that the whole approach to medical care is a lot different than that of most traditional health providers. Most free clinics feel people have a right to know what's going on with their bodies. There is much less hassle; there is much more patient involvement. There is not so much separation between the consumer and the provider, and that is just as important as its being free of charge. The aura of mystique that surrounds the medical profession is rapidly dissipated."

The Senior Citizens

Not all social activists and liberal reformers wear long hair and blue jeans. Maggie Kuhn, white-haired and close to seventy but sprightly and quick-witted as many half her age, is founder and prime mover of the Gray Panthers, a national organization of militant old people—and young. "Our society is age-ist," says Maggie. "It automatically scraps people just like old automobiles. It wants to keep the elderly out of the way, playing bingo and shuffleboard. But the subject of age affects all persons. A fetish is made of being young and keeping up youthful appearances."

Yet more than 20 million Americans are over sixty-five years of age. Though the elderly constitute one of the nation's largest reservoirs of human experience, skill, and wisdom, their talents are grossly wasted and disregarded. Society's bias against old people ignores the need for continuity and historical perspective in the current age of rapid change and rampant technology; older people have limited opportunities to contribute what they know, because they have no place or platform.

Formed in Philadelphia in early 1970, the Gray Panthers quickly attracted a large following—branches now exist in Pennsylvania, New York, Illinois, Ohio, Arizona, New Mexico, and California. The growing network of elderly activists includes many private groups, coalitions, and individuals who have the experience and strength of numbers by which to remind political parties and politicians, corporations, and religious and educational institutions of their responsibility to bear their fair share of the social costs of developing programs and services that will serve the public interest and enhance the quality of life in the United States.

Named by a television program director who thought "Gray Panthers" would lend some punch to the group's efforts at reform, from the beginning the Panthers have been oriented toward action. They are quick to distinguish themselves from those who belong to golden-age clubs which center around service or recreation, or those who cater to the elderly. "Service is fine," says Mrs. Kuhn, "but it doesn't change the system. We don't need more car pools to serve the old, we need a new type of public transportation." After the Panthers threatened to stand on the tracks and stop streetcars with their wheel chairs and canes, their calls for a better transportation system were taken more seriously. The Panthers have been equally active in taking on the banks of the Delaware Valley, and they succeeded in reforming the traditional methods for getting pension checks cashed, ordering money, and using property as collateral for loans.

Work currently in progress includes:

—Development of a new residence in West Philadelphia in the center of University City to house older and younger adults. It will be operated on a cooperative, nonprofit basis by the residents. Plans include commercial facilities for the convenience of residents, a community information center, and opportunities for social involvement with the people living near the University of Pennsylvania.

—Creation of a data bank about community resources —people, organized groups, service agencies, community concerns, and needs.

—Promotion of an Oral History Project to stimulate the acquisition and preservation of tape-recorded interview memoirs of older persons through collaborative relationships with younger people. Publication of segments of the interviews is planned.

—Analysis and critique of the present health-care situation and proposed plans for a national health program like those of Great Britain, Canada, and Scandinavia. ("We are concerned about mediocre care of the sick, the soaring costs of health insurance and hospital care, and the nondelivery of our present health system.")

—Investigation of present services and programs for older persons, their goals and methods of work. (Whom do they reach? Who runs them? How are they funded? How democratic are they? Are old people represented in determining policy and program?)

—Efforts to eliminate age discrimination and compulsory retirement on the basis of chronological age.

In late 1973, the Panthers merged with the Retired Professional Action Group. Future plans for the organization call for action on various other problems of transportation, health, taxation, and housing maintenance. The Panthers and the RPAG are especially active in advocating that older people be placed in charge of their nursing and retirement homes: organizing patients' rights committees, training people to investigate abuses, studying Medicare and other health-care programs for their cost and quality. Because housing of old people in retirement communities "ghettoizes" them and isolates the elderly from mainstream living, the group hopes to experiment with new models of housing for people of all ages (as it is doing in its West Philadelphia facility), and to develop new agreements for residents of retirement homes which would give them a voice in policy decisions.

Action will be continued to secure reduced bus and subway fares for older people, as well as to change bus routes, study mass transportation systems in various U.S. cities and Europe, and participate in public hearings on the subject. Similarly, the Panthers will continue to seek reforms in the Social Security System and in the courts. Political strategies are carefully drawn. The group supports social action in stockholders' meetings and lobbies for changes in corporate policy to benefit consumers.

The main office of the Gray Panthers and the RPAG is in a Philadelphia church. Operating funds are derived mostly from donations by church groups and individuals. There is a small paid staff. Supplementing the older staff members are a number of young people, many of whom were attracted by Maggie Kuhn's fiery rhetoric—especially her pitch that "age-ism affects both young and old, depriving both of the right to control their lives. (The first and third generations get along fine—the gaps are between the middle-aged and both groups.)"

The group often demonstrates its grievances with tactics other than marching in the streets. It does not overlook its special station. "Because of our sophistication there are many ways we can wield influence. But we must retain our integrity and dignity. I used to think that a group of us older people could get away with murder—they'd treat us with some kind of deference. But not at all. At the White House gate they were ready to knock us around just like they do the kids."

The Gray Panthers have no tight structure—there aren't any membership cards or formal offices—but there is a steering committee of fifteen people and an adopted platform for social change, a manifesto which reads in part:

> We affirm the dignity and status of age and pledge ourselves to a new life style that demonstrates the rights to self-determination and participation in determining the policy and program decisions in institutions that serve us—political party caucus groups, professional societies,

churches, synagogues, service clubs for older persons, retirement homes and committees.

We challenge arbitrary and compulsory retirement on the basis of chronological age. Such discriminatory retirement is a waste of human resources and a cause of financial hardship and loss of status and self-esteem. Older workers should have options to continue in their jobs as long as they are physically and psychologically able; to receive training for second and third careers; also to contribute to society in various voluntary groups.

We press for reforms in the present pension systems of public and private groups to assure their reliability and adequacy; and to correct the gross deficiencies and mismanagement of present systems.

We recommend that the research and development budgets of the U.S. Government agencies and bureaus be turned to designing and producing "people-serving" programs. In order for daily work to enhance the lives and spirits of our people, the products of our toil must be geared to improving the quality of our common life.

We press for a reordering of national priorities so that the manufacture of war-related material may be ended and our advanced technology be redirected to the solution of our enormous backlog of domestic problems.

We believe that our nation has the capacity to abolish poverty within our lifetime. Human dignity and liberation require adequate provision for income and employment. Therefore, we join with the National Welfare Rights organization in supporting a guaranteed annual income for all persons.

We have as our goal the redirection of national priorities so that the nation, torn by war and lack of public trust, may become just and human.

The Blood Donors

Many Americans share a growing concern about the efficiency and safety of blood-banking practices in the United States. Critics deplore the commercialism of the business —in particular the competition and lack of coordination among various banking networks, sharp variations in the costs of blood and blood products, the flimsiness of both federal and state regulatory activity, and, perhaps worst of all, sheer waste.

The most visible part of the controversy centers on the waste of money, blood, and lives. Every year, thousands of people become critically ill or die of hepatitis, a disease often caused by transfusions of virus-infected blood given by alcoholics, drug addicts, and prisoners—most of them paid donors—among whom infection is ten to seventy times more likely than in the rest of the population. Even the patient who avoids hepatitis cannot always dodge the high price of blood. One of the startling results of the present uncoordinated, nonvolunteer system has been a gross inconsistency in costs. Hospital patients are charged anywhere from $10.50 to over $100 per pint—which covers the cost of processing, repeated cross-matching, replacement, and transfusion.

The King County Central Blood Bank (Seattle, Washington) is the best organized and most effective blood bank in the United States, and it is virtually the only one of its kind. As the single, centralized, totally volunteer blood-banking facility in the Seattle area, it has decreased transfusion-induced disease to a bare minimum, and reduced costs to those only for services rendered.

For a business which at first would seem to need but a few simple rules, blood-banking has been characterized by a remarkable diversity in philosophy and organization. At issue are the sources (volunteers or paid donors), the nature of the commodity (a gift or a commercial good), and the distribution of services (centralized or decentralized). Commercial blood-bankers tend to see blood as a product, like milk, to be bought and sold; they are often opposed by those who believe that, like living tissue, blood is part of the human body and therefore not subject to the rules of trade.

The present blood-banking complex began to take shape in the 1940s. Dominating the business are the National Red Cross and the American Association of Blood Banks. The Red Cross collects from volunteers about half the national total of 7–8 million pints. The AABB, a trade association, protects the interests of the hundreds of hospital blood banks. In addition, an unknown number of commercial blood banks operate for profit—paying donors $5 to $10 per pint. Red Cross charges participating hospitals only the costs involved in processing, while the AABB feels that the only way to encourage donation is to levy a replacement fee—usually around $25—over and above the processing charges. (The fee is returned if the blood recipient can round up donors to replace the units he has received.)

Both the AABB and the Red Cross share a strong disdain for their commercial competitors. Loosely regulated and rarely prosecuted, the commercial blood banks have an unsavory reputation for buying and selling sickness and disease. Though they collect only a small percentage of the national blood supply, commercial banks do a large business in plasmapharesis (the process whereby whole blood is drawn from the donor, red blood cells are extracted and reinjected into the donor, and the plasma is retained and further separated into fractions). This procedure allows a donor to give blood as often as four times per week (in contrast to whole-blood donors, who must wait eight weeks), and permits a sizable number of people thus to earn their living. The chance that a transfused patient will contact hepatitis from the blood of paid donors is high.

What is needed, say responsible blood-bankers, are uniform standards, inspection, and accounting procedures, as well as transition to an all-volunteer system. Many agree with English sociologist Richard Titmuss (author of *The Gift Relationship*) that "no cost should be attached to the substance itself, either between donor and collector or between distributor and user."

The King County Central Blood Bank is responsible for all collection, processing, and cross-matching of blood used in Seattle hospitals. It was incorporated in 1944, by a group of businessmen and physicians, as a nonprofit organization with tax-exempt status and with provision for general community representation— anyone in the area who expresses an interest in the blood bank may become a member. The board of trustees is selected primarily from the membership. Through the years, the director, selected by the board, has served without contract or other limiting legal strictures. Successful performance of the blood bank is the criterion by which his continuation in office is determined.

The King County Central Blood Bank abides by the precepts that there should be only one organization for procuring and processing blood in the area; that the community is ultimately responsible for the blood supply to individuals who serve as volunteer donors; and that centralization of the facility, including all laboratory work necessary for transfusing blood, is essential for control of inventory and utilization.

With the appointment of a new director in 1968, several

administrative steps were taken to change the bank's operational procedures. An extensive computer system was installed to control inventory and to keep track of rare-blood donors. Educational programs for technicians, interns, residents, fellows, and participating physicians and surgeons were increased. New controls on blood utilization by physicians were developed. Vigorous cost-control measures were initiated.

A parallel development of the blood bank's social philosophy led to elimination of the traditional replacement-guarantee fee. Where formerly a $25 charge was imposed upon the individual who received blood (forcing him to assume responsibility for replacing it), now the feeling is that this responsibility does not derive from having received blood, but rather from being a member of the community. The blood bank, as an agency of the community, assumes the primary role in educating and stimulating members of the community, however organized, to provide the blood that is needed.

The bank judges its responsibilities to be as follows:

—To provide a sufficient quantity of blood and blood products to satisfy the therapeutic needs of all patients requiring treatment, regardless of a patient's ability to pay or replace the product used.

—To efficiently utilize blood from volunteer donors in order to eliminate waste in all its forms.

—To educate the medical community in the efficient and competent use of blood.

—To assure that blood and blood products will be handled in a scientifically proper way, including the elimination, insofar as possible, of blood-borne diseases, and the performance of proper laboratory identification and matching procedures.

—To keep charges to a minimum, consistent with necessary standards of quality.

By eliminating the replacement-guarantee fee, assuming total responsibility for all transfusion needs of patients, and continuing to develop scientific and research expertise, the Seattle blood-banking system stands uniquely above the country's other blood programs. Direct benefits to the Seattle community are reflected by the statistics: patients pay only $10.50 per pint of whole blood, and the rate of infectious hepatitis is something less than one per cent, and there has been no shortage of blood or its components.

The Public Researchers

It was back in 1950 that a coalition of businessmen, professionals, educators, and other civic leaders from throughout Louisiana created the Louisiana Public Affairs Research Council, a private, nonprofit organization dedicated to improving and correcting the state's basic political weaknesses. The Council still actively pursues its objective—better representative government—by helping citizens and their elected officials better *understand* the problematical issues before them. To achieve its goal the Council seeks to accumulate a substantial body of unassailable research, which it then disseminates by way of massive and effective communication to citizens and their elected representatives.

A research committee determines which issues will be investigated, and evaluates and establishes priorities among the numerous proposals submitted by staff, public officials, and private citizens. Researchers produce manuscripts for general review by the entire staff and by knowledgeable outside readers. Though most of the studies emerge with specific recommendations for solving state problems, the Council maintains its belief that the best way to achieve political change is not by way of political pressure but through deep-rooted public understanding and support; hence, it does not lobby, and there is no partisan alignment.

In addition, the group makes clear that its research is not intended for bookshelves but for the people who can and will use it effectively. Each of the reports is sent without charge to all legislators and major state and local officials. The Council also goes to great lengths to assure that the essence of its findings is made available to every home in Louisiana by way of the mass media. Publications are sent to high-school teachers of civics and social studies, to college and university professors of government and economics, and to public libraries. Council members make numerous speeches and television appearances, and lend assistance to legislative committees, trade associations, and chambers of commerce, and respond to inquiries from public officials, the press, and citizens. The Public Affairs Research Council has thus become a primary source of information on state and local problems in Louisiana.

Over the past twenty years, Council research has brought about a number of major political and governmental reforms throughout the state. Examples are:

—An August 1971 report produced an equitable reapportionment of the entire Louisiana legislature which was imposed by the United States District Court.

—A two-year study of vocational-technical education needs led to the 1973 approval by the legislature of a $54 million complex of forty-seven vocational schools throughout the state.

—A *Legislative Bulletin on Taxes* forced passage of strengthened laws to curb tax evasion.

—*Health Insurance for State Employees* encouraged development of a health and hospital-insurance plan for state public servants.

—Establishment of the offices of a Legislative Council and a Legislative Auditor followed reports issued recommending their creation.

Membership in the Louisiana Public Affairs Research Council is open to all interested citizens and to private and governmental organizations. Current full-time staff members (twenty) are paid, and the Council's activities are conducted with an annual budget of $425,000 which derives primarily from the contributions of more than 5300 members—citizens, public officials, and business firms. Donations range from $35 to $10,000 per year. Three quarters of the members pay $100 or less, and their combined contributions finance some 40 per cent of the Council's activities.

Louisiana's long history of turbulent politics has thus been mitigated by an educational and research program that reaches both the decision-makers and their constituency—providing a far greater assurance that Louisiana will find sound and lasting solutions to its state-wide problems, nurturing a more responsive government and a less apathetic citizenry than could otherwise be possible.

The Justice Monitors

The Task Force for Justice was created out of a concern by the Presbytery of New York City for social justice and action in its communities. The Presbytery recognized that many persons were being denied fundamental needs and services, that individuals had little or no effect upon institutions created to better their own lives, and that many persons and communities had no defense against institutional abuse. It was also felt that present legal and social systems seemed to lack visible and legitimate mechanisms for redress of grievances.

Also apparent was the fact that the organizations and agencies established to bring about social and legal reform and to provide due process lacked the resources to do so: the legal, social, and economic needs of New Yorkers exceeded the capacities of those charged with correcting wrongs and resolving inequities and conflicts. Likewise wanting was an effort to personalize the encounters of individuals with the controlling institutions.

An internal problem which haunted the Task Force initially was one of direction: whether to counsel the Church's parishioners, or to develop experimental projects with the expectation that they would have impact on the institutions governing New York City. In addition, because of the experimental nature of the program finally selected, concrete results were not immediately forthcoming and the program within the Presbytery decreased. The Task Force was at first unable to sustain a press relationship that made its efforts visible, and an extraordinary amount of jealousy among public-interest groups precluded them from working together.

The Presbytery decided to establish a law office—the Task Force for Justice—as a specialized form of ministry to New York City. Its purpose: to develop actions and programs which public-interest and government-funded law offices were unable to create because of the former's need to generate fees and the latter's overwhelming case loads. In order to bring about programs that would have fundamental impact on lives vis-à-vis institutions, the Task Force thought it necessary to avoid the staggering costs and time spent on litigation, unless it was a precedent-setting test case.

Initially the Task Force had one attorney, who concentrated his efforts on developing impact programing and actions in the areas of the judiciary, housing (landlord-tenant) laws, unemployment insurance, matrimonial actions, delivery of legal services to the public, and legal education of the public.

During its first eighteen months the Task Force concentrated its efforts on *amicus curiae* briefs concerning the fairness of the grand jury system, the dumping of wastes into a public estuary, and the denial of information to community health advisory boards which had been established as a prerequisite for receipt of funds by hospital corporations. Also during its initial phase, the Task Force was able to act as a conduit for funds from the federal government to develop a legal services program for the elderly poor.

Then two service-related projects were developed. The first involved securing a grant from a private foundation for use during the summer months to hire students from local law and social work schools, to aid in organizing the underemployed and unemployed in order that they might receive income supplementation such as Medicaid, food stamps, and welfare assistance. A second project adopted the policy of using nonprofessionals in delivering assistance to the inmate population of New York City's detention facilities. Visitations were instituted involving Presbytery parishioners in a one-to-one relationship with inmates; the "visitors" received training by lawyers and correctional officials, and were to act as the inmate's link to the free community. The program was established in part to awaken general public interest in the issues that had led to inmate riots a few years ago, in the belief that direct scrutiny of the prisons by the public is necessary for the political support needed for prison reform. The visitation project was jointly sponsored, allowing the Task Force to withdraw after it became viable. The Presbytery has since begun its own prison project, with grant money donated by a private party from within the Church.

A third stage of the Task Force's work evolved upon the theory that concrete step-by-step programs for public involvement in the legal system is essential to developing both ongoing public commitment and a focus of power within the community itself to effect changes. That is to say, communities must be able to challenge the system with their own resources, rather than depend upon the gratuities of government-funded legal offices which may not exist the next day. Thus, a Court Monitoring and Evaluation Project was developed which will provide data necessary to examine the operations of New York City's landlord-tenant courts and the effects of New York's housing laws upon tenants. The landlord-tenant court was selected because of its vast impact on residential housing, but its approach remained low-key. The establishment of the court program satisfied many objectives: 1) to document the routine, daily operations of a court for purposes of legislative improvement; 2) to demonstrate the public's concern for a properly functioning judicial system; 3) to educate citizens about and guide them step-by-step into the system; 4) to create a forum for the public to speak out when so moved; and 5) to establish an ongoing office as an alternative to the methods used by the New York State judiciary to police its own personnel and enforce uniform standards. The type of data and the method of collection are unique to court studies, most of which are done solely for managerial purposes and not to determine how the operations of the courts affect the parties and whether the "laws" actually accomplish what they were designed to do.

Monitors, extensively trained in housing law and procedure and using data questionnaires drawn by the Task Force, worked in teams of two during morning and evening sessions of the court, five days a week. Over 90 per cent of the monitors were college students from schools in the metropolitan area, and they received credit for their efforts on the project. Of disappointment to the Task Force was a general lack of response from the many civic and community groups that had been invited to participate.

The Task Force for Justice was instrumental in organizing a number of tenants' associations into a coalition to fight for specific legislation for a proposed Housing Court act. In its first major effort to effect housing laws, it arranged a series of press conferences and releases, public meetings, sessions with legislators, mass mailings to city and state officials, testimony before a judicial panel, and, most important, legislative workshops which drafted new laws. The group then joined in a suit against the Civil Court's administrative judge for failing to comply with the new Housing Court laws by not appointing true representatives of tenants' groups to an advisory counsel.

Shortly after the court project was launched, the Task Force began to investigate numerous complaints that had been brought to its attention regarding the New York City

Unemployment Insurance system: its lack of due process protections and its bureaucratic indifference to claimants. It found that the unemployment offices often discouraged claimants from utilizing assistance, although many needed basic legal information to enable them to receive benefits. The Task Force recommended two remedies: a city-wide legal assistance office, and the publication of a strategy manual for claimants to aid them in obtaining benefits. Then it proceeded to write the manual.

Another project undertaken by the Task Force concerned ways by which new systems of delivering legal services could be developed, and which could easily be replicated by other organizations. It chose to set up a matrimonial law office, to provide counseling on the legal and social-psychological aspects of marriage or divorce by an interdisciplinary staff of attorneys, paralegal assistants, and social workers.

In order to deliver legal services at a decreased cost per case, paralegal professionals are assigned to the unemployment insurance and matrimonial projects.

Overall, the philosophy of the Task Force remains to develop programs which bring about a greater increase in services, rather than merely to study problems and make recommendations to generally unresponsive bodies with no real interest in reforms.

As Professionals

The Public Accountants

Accountants for the Public Interest was formed in 1971 with the express purpose of establishing a structure within the accounting profession that would provide investigative, nonadvocative accounting counsel, without fee, to other nonprofit organizations serving the public interest. It is the first and only such organization in the country.

The founding members were individual San Francisco/ Bay Area accountants and educators each of whom feel that the accounting profession has a broad responsibility to society which is not being adequately fulfilled: accountants, uniquely qualified to serve the public as the only professionals educated, trained, and recognized specifically for their independence and objectivity, were falling short of satisfying the frequent need for accounting advice in public-interest studies, cases, and projects presently being conducted by community-oriented groups.

The public-interest accountants' clients are typically either legal, community, or consumer organizations which have projects or cases involving public-interest matters with financial or accounting implications. Dealing mostly with published documents, items of public record, or data submitted by defendants in lawsuits, the volunteer CPAs organize and interpret such information, and report their findings, thus balancing with accounting data and terminology the professional advice available to the opposing party. When the occasion warrants, they appear in court or before legislative or regulatory agencies. Traditional

accounting or tax services for clients' own internal affairs
are not performed.

One of the first cases in which Accountants for the Public Interest took part involved the National Health and Environmental Law Program, an OEO-funded group that had
filed suit in federal court in New Orleans against three
hospitals which had received federal funds (under the
Hill-Burton Act) in return for providing, among other
things, "a reasonable volume of free services to persons
unable to pay." The services were to be contingent upon
the hospitals' "financial feasibility" (a term used without
definition in the Act). This would be the first in a series of
suits being filed in districts around the country in an
attempt to enforce the requirements of the Hill-Burton
Act. The public-interest accountants evaluated the data
and issued a report on the question of "financial feasibility" which was utilized by the presiding district court
judge in a precedent-setting decision that required the
New Orleans hospitals to provide a *specified* degree of free
services to the poor.

Other cases handled by Accountants for the Public Interest have included:

—Analysis of financial data for the proposed Yerba
Buena Redevelopment Center (client, San Francisco
Neighborhood Legal Assistance).

—Estimation of the effect on San Francisco's budget,
and on consumer utility bills, of a proposed municipal
acquisition of certain Pacific Gas & Electric Co. utility
properties (client, San Francisco Neighborhood Legal
Assistance in conjunction with Citizens for Public Power).

—Consultations and investigations related to rate increases sought by both Pacific Telephone and Pacific Gas
& Electric Co. (client, San Francisco Consumer Action).

In addition, the accountants analyzed costs and operations of two Farm Labor Centers in connection with a rent increase proposed by the Tulare County Housing Authority, and testified before a federal district court judge in an action brought by California Rural Legal Assistance for an injunction, an involvement that contributed to a reduction in the requested increase and to the impounding of granted increases by the court pending its final decision. They have also studied various financial problems of the San Francisco Unified School District. Said the API's client in that case, the San Francisco Parent-Teacher Association: "First they gave us factual information regarding the language and mechanics of accounting. But they also gave us the confidence to speak up and ask questions about school money—our money."

As its reputation grows, so do the number of clients served by the volunteer CPAs. The group has been retained by the Youth Law Center to study the costs and financing related to emergency care of dependent and neglected children in San Francisco, in connection with a plan to develop alternative and comprehensive treatment facilities. For the San Francisco Lawyers' Committee on Urban Affairs, the accountants are helping to formulate plans to include low- and moderate-income housing in a large proposed development in San Mateo County. The San Francisco Ecology Center has asked for a review of the financial elements in a proposed $390 million expansion to San Francisco's International Airport; the Coalition of San Francisco Neighborhoods has requested assistance in development of model forms and practices that could be used in local elections so that interested citizens can intelligently evaluate how campaign funds have been handled. Other organizations, such as the Mexican-American Legal Defense and Education Fund, the American Civil Liberties Union, San

Francisco Equal Employment Opportunities Project, the Environmental Defense Fund, and the Council on Municipal Performance have also inquired as to the availability of accounting services.

Accountants for the Public Interest currently consists of about thirty-five board members and volunteers, committed to lending their professional expertise to those who have had little access to independent, objective accounting and data analysis. The organization rents two small rooms in an old office building in the heart of San Francisco's business district. Control is vested in a board of twenty-one directors. Acceptance of assignments and approval of reports are made by an executive committee composed of seven certified public accountants. The current paid staff consists of Morton Levy, one of the group's founders and its half-time executive director, and one full-time secretary. Incorporated in 1972 as a nonprofit California enterprise, the public-interest accountants take pains to inform related professional groups—the San Francisco Chapter of the California Society of CPAs, the California Society of CPAs, and the American Institute of CPAs—of their activities.

Although it was funded solely by foundations in its first and second years, API is exploring a variety of plans for permanent financing. They include general appeals to the profession, solicitation of businesses for the funding of specific projects, and receipt of fees from public-interest law firm clients through the medium of court-ordered cost reimbursements to be paid by losing parties in class action suits.

Accountants for the Public Interest attempts to provide answers for clients and problems that heretofore could not have been handled professionally, either because of limited access or limited funds. The group utilizes accounting student assistants from local colleges and universities, in

an effort to spur bright young students who have an awareness of their social responsibility into entering the profession. From the beginning, the public-interest accountants
in San Francisco have recognized their obligation to
encourage the formation of similar organizations elsewhere in the country; 20 per cent of the group's budget
has been applied to this cause. It has sponsored a national
public-interest accounting conference which was attended
by CPAs from all over the country. As a result, other
autonomous organizations are being formed in other cities
around the United States, a national committee has been
formed to plan and coordinate future activities, and a
national public accounting newsletter is being published.

Some accountants have expressed concern over the possibility that their public-interest colleagues would have a
difficult time upholding the profession's cherished code of
objectivity when they identify so closely with their sometimes anti-Establishment, often politically active clients.
But Levy says that any of his group's undertakings are on a
strictly professional basis, and unbiased. "The only way
we can separate ourselves from the advocacy role of our
clients is through our work product."

It is difficult to forecast how well a traditionally conservative profession will receive groups like Accountants for
the Public Interest, but this much is certain: the need for
public-interest accounting services has been well demonstrated. There is much more to be done.

The Scientists

Operating on a minuscule budget but engaged in a whirl of important activity, the Center for Science in the Public Interest presents the technical information that special interests and their governmental regulatory agencies frequently choose to ignore. The Center also seeks to offer an alternative professional style for scientists and engineers. Such efforts are especially important in a city where thousands of health and safety issues are debated and policy decisions made every day.

The group is controlled by three men—Ph.D.s with backgrounds in meteorology and oceanography, organic chemistry, and biochemistry—all working for far less pay than they could command in government or industry. They share the feeling that too many scientists, in trying to preserve the purity of their work, deliberately avoid making judgments regarding the public welfare and often fall into the role of playing advocate for the particular interest of their employers. A different kind of advocacy, it is argued, should be forthcoming from scientists, one based on thorough consideration of the implications of their research: each should assess the social impact of his own work. Because most laboratories have vested interests in their research, many scientists are either unaware or confused about their ethical and moral responsibilities. Through careful research and study, the Center's staff has demonstrated that national policies are set not by concern for the public's best interests but by bureaucratic inertia and thirst for profits.

In its efforts to encourage the application of science and

technology to the solution of environmental problems, and to spur scientists themselves "to work purposefully and aggressively in the public interest," the Center is currently engaged in various writing and research activities. One is to make available competent witnesses to testify at hearings on science-related legislation pending before Congress. Staff members recently testified before the Senate Commerce Committee's Subcommittee on the Environment, deploring excessive delay by the Environmental Protection Agency in issuing inner-city air pollution standards. Evidence was presented that the urban poor are exposed to four and five times as high carbon-monoxide levels as suburban residents.

Another activity is to supply consumers with information on matters about which data are either unavailable or obscured by conflicting facts. Reports are issued at low cost. Publications issued to date have included "Chemical Additives in Booze," "Fluorides in the Air," "The Stripping of Appalachia," "Asbestos and You," "How Sodium Nitrite Can Affect Your Health," and critical analyses—in terms understandable to laypersons—of food colorings and gasoline additives. The three founders of the Center have each written books during their short tenures. Albert Fritsch (an ordained Jesuit priest with a doctorate in organic chemistry) authored *A Theology of the Earth*, Michael Jacobson (whose doctorate is in biochemistry) wrote *Eater's Digest* and *Nutrition Scoreboard*, and James Sullivan (whose doctorate is in meteorology and oceanography) is completing work on *Evaluating Highway Environmental Impacts*.

The Center's methods are to produce information for the public on the scientific and technical implications of products, policies, and phenomena, to train students, and to organize alliances with citizen groups. The Center also instigates its own public-interest lawsuits or serves as co-plaintiff—as it did when it joined the Natural Resources Defense Council in an action charging the EPA with using faulty test procedures in setting the standard for hydrocarbon emissions from automobile tail pipes. Along with the Consumer Federation of America and the Federation of Homemakers, the Center charged that the Food and Drug Administration has failed to enforce its own regulations requiring retailers to post notice if a package label does not include artificial coloring. The Center also helped develop information charging that the USDA allows the potentially hazardous food additive sodium nitrite to be used, even when it is not necessary.

Since its founding in 1971, the Center for Science in the Public Interest has been operating on a few small grants from foundations. In the future, it expects to rely heavily on contributions from the public, which it solicits through a quarterly newsletter that spills the beans on, among other things, what's going on in federal regulatory agencies. Items from a recent issue include a warning about nitrosamines ("Don't bring home the bacon—it's probably the most dangerous food available"), a listing of food additives that are widely used but have not been adequately tested (such as violet dye in candies and soda water), and documentation of the dangers related to asbestos ("which is widely used in brake linings, ironing-board pads, insulation" and "can cause lung cancer and other crippling and fatal illnesses"). Many such pieces are developed into "countercommercials" (see Public Interest Communications, Inc. and Public Communication, Inc.), which are broadcast over various radio stations across the country.

From its headquarters in a sparsely furnished row house, the Center seeks "to stoke the social consciences of scientists, and to establish the legitimacy of their acting

in the public interest." After all, it argues, there is no
such thing as complete scientific objectivity—all scientists
make value judgments—and it is patently unethical to
withhold pertinent research data from the public.

The Businessmen

The idea that business has duties to the public beyond its own production and profit-making is an ancient concept, long embodied in the law. The earliest codes contained provisions establishing standards of weights and measures, fixing prices for goods and charges for services, and attempting to protect the public against scarcity and overreaching. Through the centuries, the obligation of business to the community has broadened; the old rule of *caveat emptor*, let the buyer beware, is gradually giving way to various theories of implied warranty. And some businessmen themselves are assuming increased social responsibility.

Business and Professional People for the Public Interest (know as BPI) combines into one Chicago center a law firm, research center, and agency of ombudsmen. A nonprofit corporation, whose members are business and professional people, BPI works toward relieving the poor, relaxing neighborhood tensions, halting community deterioration, and defending civil and human rights—in short, toward better citizenship.

BPI's full-time staff concerns itself exclusively with the quality of life in the Chicago metropolitan area. Through lawyers, research associates, and a board of directors comprised of representatives from among the forty Chicago business concerns that help pay part of the group's $300,-000 annual budget, the organization has charted a two-pronged approach to solving problems: action-oriented research, and litigation designed to bring about substantive change.

BPI sponsors continuing and intensive analysis of industrial pollution along Lake Michigan, monitoring all companies that apply for permits to discharge wastes into the water, and issues reports on the amount and content of such effluents to the public and to the Environmental Protection Agency. It also prepares separate studies of health hazards caused by toxic substances dumped into the lake.

Other research activities cover investigations into bonding practices in criminal courts, juvenile court proceedings, the Cook County Coroner's Office, and the Chicago Police Department. Some of the research is done in conjunction with the Center for Urban Affairs of Northwestern University and the Northwestern University Law School.

A major portion of BPI's legal activity has been to halt environmental degradation, but the group has also litigated such matters as Illinois' criminal abortion laws, racial discrimination in Chicago's largest commercial high school, favoritism in tax assessment, fee-splitting, and the selection of sites for public housing. The businessmen have won impressive victories on the environmental front, including:

—A decision against the Consumer Power Company of Michigan which led to construction of cooling towers at its Palisades Nuclear Plant, thus eliminating that source of thermal pollution of Lake Michigan.

—An order requiring U.S. Steel to eliminate or substantially reduce particulate matter from its 829 coke ovens in Gary, Indiana.

—Acknowledgment by the Atomic Energy Commission of the seriousness of design defects in the emergency cooling systems at nuclear power plants.

In urban affairs, BPI has issued reports on integrity in government, administration of criminal justice, housing policies and practices, First Amendment abuses, and the lawyer's role. BPI weighs each case for its potential to bring about institutional change. Thus a suit involving Illinois race-track scandals did not merely seek to pin liability on individuals, but also to change the state law on fiduciary responsibility of public officials. A complaint against the Army Corp of Engineers and the EPA was intended not only to remedy pollution emanating from one plant but to achieve higher control standards for the entire area. Likewise, a petition against the Cook County Assessor's Office— long notorious for special deals and arbitrary practices— sought fundamental reforms and procedures for public review.

While BPI is proud of its successes, it recognizes the battles still ahead. Like most public-interest organizations, the Chicago group is plagued by the difficult and time-consuming skirmishes to get information and to obtain funds. Original support and organizing impetus came in 1969 from Gordon Sherman, then president of Midas-International, who advocated a full-time public-interest legal and research firm. Sherman supported his primary contention—that it is the duty of corporations to be socially responsible—with generous contributions from the Midas-International Foundation. During 1973, private business contributed one third of BPI's operating budget. Most of the backers are executives of smaller companies, but they represent a wide spectrum of the business community— among them hotel executives, retailers, investment brokers, small manufacturers, and bankers.

Why do business and professional people join an organization which has already embarrassed Illinois' largest corporations and community leaders? Because they believe it is in their own best interest, as members of the community, to do so. "The power companies have often been our customers," says the president of an automotive supply company, "and I know what the BPI is doing in pollution control could cost them a lot of money. But, if we're motivated only be fear, then we're missing what this country really stands for."

Alexander Polikoff, BPI's executive director, sums up the group's *raison d'être*: "We think it important that there be a vehicle in the community for responsible social action by concerned business, and that it be a vehicle for which business has special responsibility. There is room and an important role for groups like BPI—not tied to government, not supported by major private institutions, unburdened with institutional responsibilities or selfish interests—representative of, and free to represent, the morals and ideals of America."

The Economists

Economists have joined the public-interest movement. Economic forces and their underlying cultural bases contribute in large measure to the social and environmental problems which afflict American and world society, and the present distribution of economic power greatly impedes their solution. These inequities are compounded by the uneven availability of knowledge. Thus, in policy debates, advocates of the public interest often lack access to economic data, and informed and rational public dialogue on policy choices and goals is often impossible. While the private interest is amply represented in legislative, judicial, and regulatory proceedings, and impressed on public opinion through the various media, the general welfare is frequently neglected. Those most affected by the outcome —the aged, the poor, workers, women, minorities, consumers—often lack the power and resources to compete effectively in the political and judicial arenas. Similarly, the need to protect and maintain a healthy physical environment has been discounted in many policy decisions.

In recent years, the emergence of other public-interest groups with wider perspectives has led to more vigorous assertion of the general welfare. All of them share a growing understanding that economics must be translated into terms more intelligible to concerned laymen; much economic writing and analysis has been politically irrelevant, overly academic, too costly, or otherwise unavailable to citizen groups—especially at the grass-roots level.

Public-interest organizations have had no regular access to reliable economic advice on a *pro bono* basis, nor has there been organized interaction between citizen or consumer constituencies and the economics profession. Many activists do not fully perceive the links between economic policies and their particular constituencies and goals. The impact of policies involving taxation, international trade and development, employment, monopoly regulation, and agriculture on such public concerns as the presentation of urban vitality and environmental quality has rarely been assessed.

To meet these manifold needs, a group of economists and public-interest organizers established the Public Interest Economics Center in May 1972 and, soon thereafter, the Public Interest Economics Foundation. Both are located in Washington, D.C. The Center performs grant or contract research, all of which must meet stringent public-interest criteria, as well as *pro bono* work on particularly urgent issues. It presents and facilitates testimony by highly qualified economists at all levels of government, addressing such public-interest considerations as the redistribution of income and wealth, protection of the biosphere, the shifting of economic priorities, and reduction of economic waste. The Foundation, on the other hand, is designed as a publicly supported group with tax-deductible status. It conducts educational programs for noneconomists —policy-makers, professionals in other areas, civic and community leaders, and the general public. It also performs such economic-policy research as can be undertaken by a corporation with its tax status.

The goals of the two institutions are both general and specific:

—To provide economic advice and information to public-interest groups and to consult with them, as appropriate, in the formulation of their positions.

—To identify economists who can and will serve as ad-

visers to public-interest organizations and to facilitate the
linkage of professional economic specialists with appropriate advocacy groups.

—To facilitate two-way communication between professional economists and public-interest advocates, with the
twin aims of apprising economists of the needs for their
competence in public-interest advocacy and of informing
citizen constituencies of the relevance of general economic
reform to their particular social objectives.

—To create a professional center for economists and
for students of economics interested in public-interest
work and to provide a variety of administrative and in-
formational services to them.

—To cooperate with other public-interest professional
organizations in such fields as science, law, health care,
design, planning, communications, and human rights in
efforts to bring integrated multidisciplinary perspectives
to bear on public issues.

An advisory group of prominent economists has been
organized to further the development of public-interest
economics within the profession. This "Board of Economic
Advisers" helps formulate professional standards for
public-interest work, identify the public issues most
critically in need of both qualified analysis and of representation by public-interest economics, and reach other
qualified economists interested in effective participation
in public policy.

Economists as a group have been slow to offer their
expertise in any systematic way to fill the gap created by
mercantile and political imbalances. But there is almost
always available to private interest (with money) expert
economic consultation, advice, and analysis. The Public
Interest Economics Center, and its sister Foundation, seek
to bridge that gap.

The Lawyers:
In the Public Interest

"If courts are not a legitimate channel for achieving change," says lawyer Sidney Wolinsky, "what is? As a practical matter, legislative bodies have become, not representatives of public will, but of special-interest groups which make it very difficult for them to respond to the public interest. Thank G-d, the oil interests cannot lobby the federal judges."

In 1971, Governor Ronald Reagan vetoed federal funding for California Rural Legal Assistance, and the Nixon Administration began expressing opposition to aggressive Legal Services programs. Shortly thereafter, four young attorneys in San Francisco started thinking about setting up an independent and, it was hoped, self-sustaining public-interest law firm. They were convinced that successful advocacy for the poor, which frequently involves litigation against local, state, and federal agencies, could never be effectively funded by the federal government, and they realized that private law firms could not be expected to undertake a significant amount of law-reform cases on behalf of minorities and the poor—since such cases are often complex and enormously expensive to maintain. They believed, however, that the practice of law in the public interest would remain relatively meaningless without substantial involvement of the private bar.

The young lawyers were Anthony Kline, once chief litigating attorney for the OEO-funded National Housing and Development Law Project; Robert Gnaizda, a specialist in rural, farm-worker, hunger, and employment problems;

William H. Hasite, Jr., a prominent young black lawyer
in California; and Sidney Wolinsky, former director of
litigation in the San Francisco Neighborhood Legal Assistance Foundation. Each had spent several years in private
practice with well-known private firms before shifting his
commitment exclusively to public-interest litigation.

In September 1971 they established Public Advocates,
Inc. Their express purposes: to provide legal assistance to
those who cannot themselves afford counsel in complex law-
reform cases, and to demonstrate to the legal profession
that such a practice can be at least self-supporting if not
profitable (and should therefore not be shunned).

To accomplish this objective the group set out to challenge the general rule in this country that attorneys' fees
are normally not recoverable as costs by victorious litigants. Public Advocates figured that it would take several
years for appellate courts to begin adopting a different
view, that the issue could not be raised until some important cases were first won, and that the cases they had in
mind were complex and time-consuming. Seed money was
required to finance activities before the firm could begin
seeking fees from unsuccessful defendants. The Ford Foundation responded with interest and funds, after the group
itself had raised some $50,000 from several small Califor-
nia foundations (to demonstrate local support).

One of the most significant cases in Public Advocates'
early history was *La Raza Unida & The Sierra Club* v.
Volpe, less for its success on behalf of 5000 Mexican-
Americans whose community would be destroyed by a new
freeway, than in its precedent-shattering aftermath.
Having won an injunction against construction of the
highway, Public Advocates asked the U.S. District Court to
direct the defendant state-highway officials to pay both its
legal fees and the fees of expert witnesses. The court not
only granted the motion but based its decision on grounds

that would justify payment of a winning plaintiff's fees by a defendant in a vast array of other public-interest cases. This decision, which has received a great deal of attention within the legal profession and has already been followed by other federal and state courts, is certain to decrease the dependence of public-interest lawyers on foundation grants and to diminish the unwillingness of private attorneys to represent those who cannot afford legal fees. The court held that because lawyers like those in Public Advocates act as "private attorneys general" who "effectuate strong Congressional policies" that would otherwise remain unenforced, and thereby confer "substantial benefits" on large numbers of people, they should be paid by the government agencies that violated the law. The court went on to note that to deny them fees and force them to bear their own costs would, in effect, improperly penalize those who have vindicated important public rights.

Public Advocates was satisfied with the victory and understood its implications. "If this theory continues to be adopted by courts across the country," Tony Kline pointed out, "it can substantially diminish financial barriers that now inhibit citizens from going to court to challenge violations of law by powerful government agencies and corporate interests." Since its victory in *La Raza Unida*, Public Advocates has been awarded fees in successful suits on employment discrimination in municipal fire and police departments, prisoners' rights, and environmental protection, and hopes to be awarded fees in a variety of other cases it has recently won in federal and state courts in California.

Still, the seeking of attorneys' fees is not a primary purpose of the firm. One of Public Advocates' guiding principles has been that public-interest lawyers should confine themselves to clients who are denied access to the existing legal system. This includes not only minorities and the poor but a large portion of the middle class as well: those who are aggrieved by the actions of a giant corporation or government agency and are unable to litigate on an individual basis. Public Advocates therefore seldom takes on welfare cases (already handled by OEO legal services), nor, as a rule, does the firm accept purely environmental lawsuits sponsored by organizations with adequate financial means to pay lawyers (if they do not already have them free).

Another goal is to create coalitions between and among different types of community organizations. Such amalgams are invariably more powerful than a single plaintiff and, moreover, engender a large amount of mutual education that has long-term positive effects. Public Advocates has represented, for example, a number of minority groups opposed to the physical destruction of a community by a proposed urban renewal or highway project; in many such cases various conservationist groups have joined in as co-plaintiffs. The coalitions have not only sensitized white, upper-class people to the desperate housing needs of blacks and Chicanos, but have educated minority citizens about the environmental depredations of government agencies and the manner in which this affects them. In *La Raza Unida & The Sierra Club* v. *Volpe* the firm succeeded in stopping a $100-million highway project in Alameda County that would have displaced over 5000 low-income Mexican-Americans and destroyed three parks.

Various minority groups and eleven conservationist organizations combined in *Lathan* v. *Volpe* to halt construction of a $350-million interstate highway near Seattle which would have dissipated the largest black community in the Pacific Northwest and severely affected the ecology of Lake Washington. And in *Keith* v. *Volpe* the National Association for the Advancement of Colored People joined with the Environmental Defense Fund and the Sierra Club to block the proposed Century Freeway, a $500-million freeway that would have passed through Watts and further increased the air pollution in the Los Angeles basin. Coalitions are of course not limited to highway cases. In *Peninsula Commuter and Transit Committee et al.* v. *Public Utilities Commission*, the Mexican-American Political Association participated in an attack on regressive utility-rate structures that tend to reward heavy consumption of scarce energy resources, besides levying greater per-unit charges for power on the poor than on the more affluent. Similarly, the California Council of Older Americans joined with the Black Panthers (in *Black Panthers* v. *Kehoe*) to enforce the California Freedom of Information Act in a consumer case.

Virtually all cases filed by Public Advocates are class actions, taxpayer suits, or other representative litigations on behalf of statewide and local community organizations. In *NAACP* v. *All Regulated Public Utilities*, a single lawsuit resulted in some 25,000 additional jobs for minorities and women in management positions, together with an increase of $400 million per annum in salaries. Besides representing a large number of small community groups with local interests (ranging from a single substantive area, like cable television or education, to broader environmental issues), Public Advocates supplies legal support on a continuing basis to the NAACP (Western Region), the Mexican-American Political Association, Chinese for Affirmative Action, the League of United Latin American Citizens, the California Prisoners Union, the National Organization for Women, the Black Panther Party, the California Council of Older Americans, the United Filipino Association, United Native Americans, Inc., Self-Help for the Elderly, Inc., and Black Women Organized for Action.

A persistent problem encountered by Public Advocates' lawyers is how to choose from among the cases they are asked to take. At present they are able to handle only about 10 per cent of the suits proffered. All are chosen on the basis of the relative importance of the public interest involved, the inability of the client to retain competent private counsel, the absence of other legal agencies to provide representation, the degree to which a particular area of the law has not been adequately explored, opportunities for legal innovation, the firm's competence in the subject area, and room for participation by law students affiliated with the firm.

All of the senior lawyers in the firm came out of the OEO Legal Services Program, where they represented only the poor and the racially oppressed. OEO guidelines prohibited litigation on behalf of anyone whose income exceeded the level of hard-core poverty. Public Advocates, Inc., has no such restriction, and this is a valuable freedom in light of the fact that many middle-income citizens find legal help difficult to afford. Moreover, there are certain valid public-interest cases that must be brought by relatively affluent plaintiffs. For example, a suit to compel a corporation to hire minorities or to cease polluting a river should in some instances be filed as a stockholder derivative action, and stockholders are almost by definition not poor.

As it turns out, Public Advocates represents mostly poor clients. But a difficulty inherent in this type of constituency is that the lawyer is usually not a member of the community he represents. He may not fully understand the group's social values or political goals, and he may consciously or subconsciously seek a purely legal victory that is intellectually appealing but of small practical significance. The role of the public-interest lawyer, the attorneys at Public Advocates maintain, is not directly to address the basic political problem but rather to deal with only that part susceptible to resolution within the legal process. In so doing he must remain sensitive to and be guided by his clients' interests and desires. "This is frequently a problem when the client is not paying and the lawyer is highly educated, strongly motivated, and idealistic," says Kline. "It becomes particularly acute when the client and lawyer do not share the same class and racial background." One way in which Public Advocates tries to deal with ethnic differences is to spend as much time as possible attending meetings of client organizations, trying to understand their perhaps differing perspectives, and refraining from the presumption that a lawsuit is the only answer. When litigation is filed, strong efforts are made to involve clients in the development of strategy. In addition, from its beginning the firm has recruited attorneys (there are now eight) and other staff who are themselves members of the racial and ethnic minorities served by the firm, or who are bilingual. Of a current staff total of sixteen, ten are black, Mexican-American, or Asian, and five can speak and write Spanish. "Our firm does not plan to grow much larger than it already is," says Kline, "since such growth would involve more institutionalization than we want. Our desire is rather to remain a close-knit litigating law firm that can relate to and identify with its clients."

Ironically, another difficulty derives from the expertise and reputation that began to develop with the firm's early successes: a disinclination to explore other legal areas with which the lawyers were not so familiar. Thus, for example, as a result of its stunning victories in a half-dozen major highway suits, Public Advocates was deluged with requests from across the nation to take on more road-building cases. Though such litigation would have been relatively easy, it would have foreclosed involvement in other public-interest territories. The firm therefore adopted a policy of refusing to act as chief counsel in additional highway cases, but agrees to serve as co-counsel to local lawyers.

Public Advocates attempts to explore novel legal concepts, even though the time involved in such cases is almost prohibitive. It takes less than a week for the firm to prepare an employment-discrimination suit; but it required almost six months of preparation just to file *Serrano* v. *Priest*, the first school-financing case in U.S. history. Moreover, the trial in *Serrano* took over six months and cost the Advocates nearly $50,000.

One of the firm's longest-running cases, which it took on in 1971 and settled in late 1973, was *Tenants and Owners Opposed to Redevelopment* v. *The U.S. Department of Housing & Urban Development*. Tenants and Owners in Opposition to Redevelopment was a community organization representing over 4000 elderly men (and some women) who live in a large skid-row area of San Francisco. On that spot the city planned to build one of the most expensive commercial urban renewal projects in the country, costing about $400 million (with a bond issuance of $225 million, second largest in history). But the proposal necessitated demolition of 4000 low-cost living units, and no replacement housing was planned. Public Advocates filed suit in federal court and obtained an injunction prohibiting displacement of the residents until the San Francisco Redevelopment Agency (the main defendant) complied with federal statutes requiring that "decent, safe, and sanitary" relocation housing be provided residents at rents within their financial means. The city and HUD tried repeatedly thereafter to have the injunction dissolved or modified, on the theory that adequate relocation housing already existed. Public Advocates successfully opposed these efforts, arguing that, as is typically the case with urban-renewal plans, the city would force the displaced residents into already overcrowded ghetto housing and thereby exacerbate an existing housing crisis in San Francisco. The project had planned to build 276 units (a net reduction of over 3700 units) to go with its high-rise office building, a sports arena, and a huge underground parking lot. By April 1973 the delay in construction caused by the injunction was costing the city $1 million a month. A settlement agreement was signed, under which the city consented to build at least 2000 new or rehabilitated units of low-cost housing in and near the urban-renewal project area, to subsidize the rents on all of these units and bring them within the financial means of Public Advocates' clients, to give TOOR the right to choose the architects for the new buildings and have veto control over architectural plans, and to give the clients the right to manage the completed housing projects. The value of this settlement has been estimated by the City of San Francisco to be $152 million. The resolution of *TOOR* v. *HUD* thus benefited the entire city (helping to ease the housing crisis in the Bay Area) and helped in the political organization of the client community. In addition, the court subsequently awarded attorneys fees to the plaintiffs.

Public Advocates, Inc., aspires to continue winning a high percentage of innovative lawsuits that are both meaningful to clients and advance a significant public interest, reasoning that such victories will vindicate the relevance of the judicial process to groups heretofore denied ready access to lawyers and the courts, and successfully demonstrate that this type of legal practice can be financially self-supporting.

The Lawyers: In the Ghetto

When the prestigious Baltimore law firm of Piper and Marbury opened a neighborhood branch office in late 1969, it was not in just any neighborhood—but in a dilapidated, overcrowded, crime-ridden, underemployed section, far from the handsome executive suites where the firm has conducted a well-heeled corporate and commercial practice for more than half a century.

Piper and Marbury's branch office represents a commitment to provide the poor and disadvantaged with high-quality legal services at little or no charge. Though the neighborhood branch is still experimental, and while it is clear that no one model will be right for all inner-city communities, Piper and Marbury's efforts serve as an example of what *can* be done by the legal establishment if it is sincere in fulfilling its social responsibility. The Baltimore firm's experience also demonstrates the frustrations, problems, and conflicts that may be incurred and possibly avoided.

Piper and Marbury vetoed other alternatives for public-service involvement in favor of a separate and distinct neighborhood branch. It recognized the community's well-founded skepticism of the private bar, and felt that the substantial symbolic significance of an unobtrusive ghetto office outweighed the likely disadvantages: a potentially high case load and the inefficient use of resources occasioned by physical and psychological distance from the main office.

The branch office is located above a drugstore in an old

building on Wolfe Street, part of a predominantly black ghetto area in East Baltimore. A small sign directs clients to the second floor. Though $10,000 worth of redecorating and renovation have made the office presentable, the overall effect is intentionally low key.

The branch is staffed by two attorneys, one with past experience in legal services and the other, a more senior associate, rotated from the downtown office. Both are considered full-fledged members of the parent firm, accorded equal status and identical resources. Their work is supplemented by that of the other associates, who occasionally consult in their areas of expertise. In the Wolfe Street branch's first three years, main-office attorneys contributed free close to 500 hours in otherwise billable time. Operating expenses—around $60,000 per year—are borne by the parent office.

Greater participation from the main office has, unfortunately, been deterred by a constant stream of work from paying clients, a reluctance to give up other *pro bono* activities for the branch, and restrained enthusiasm for the branch. Some partners feel that the minimal involvement of the main office, combined with the physical detachment and directorship by a junior associate rather than a partner, reinforces a sense of isolation and psychological distance.

Fulfilling its objective to provide quality legal services, the branch handles cases with unusual care, thoroughness, and expertise. To do so, the office sacrifices quantity for quality. In its first two years the branch opened 148 cases —113 civil and 35 criminal—an average of 6.2 per month. This has meant excluding most domestic and some criminal cases, and all matters an attorney would take on a contingency basis. A somewhat ironic consequence of the high-quality–low-quantity approach is a relatively enormous expense in time, energy, and service: the average case costs Piper and Marbury $400 to $500—in contrast to the $30 expended by the Baltimore Legal Aid Bureau.

Virtually the entire civil docket of the Wolfe Street office consists of cases similar to those accepted by OEO legal services. To keep its work load manageable, a variety of complex legal issues are extracted from situations which at first appear routine; many matters are pursued beyond the limits of the initial controversy. As a result, substantial work is done in reforming the law while providing services to individual clients. Yet the branch can legitimately boast that, in nearly every case it handles, clients' problems are resolved to their satisfaction.

Actions on behalf of a class (i.e., a group of litigants with a particular grievance) are evaluated formally. Advance approval is required from the parent firm before any such action is supported. To date, such approval has been given in all matters involving injunctive relief; class actions for money damages are viewed with skepticism— perhaps because they threaten Piper and Marbury's large commercial practice.

Although the Wolfe Street office has begun to make a favorable impact upon the community, it has not fared so well with the local bar. The Ethics Committee of the Baltimore City Bar Association has overtly inhibited Piper and Marbury from realizing one of its stated goals—to encourage other firms to open neighborhood offices—by charging that the publicity attending the branch has violated the canons of legal ethics that pertain to advertising and solicitation. The Bar's Executive Committee, however, in an act of apparently superficial generosity, concluded that the publicity which came when the branch was opened was not solicited by the firm. Meanwhile the Monumental Bar Association—composed exclusively of black attorneys— questioned a white firm's ability to work effectively in the black community and expressed a concern that the branch would steal business from reputable black lawyers in the neighborhood. Although such charges smack patently of economic (rather than social or ethical) reservations, Piper and Marbury is now very reluctant to say anything about its Wolfe Street operation.

Another problem is that the branch is often forced to deal with thorny conflict-of-interest problems. Such matters are handled on an *ad hoc* basis—with little predisposition to resolve them in favor of branch- or main-office clients. However, since most main-office clients retain the firm as general counsel and therefore offer a continuing flow of legal work, some inclination exists, perhaps, to reject the branch-office client.

The fact that Piper and Marbury's neighborhood branch has not produced the perfect approach to delivering services to the poor should not obscure the central feature of the experiment—for four years a private firm has devoted a substantial portion of its resources to the full-time practice of poverty law—nor should it conceal the real benefits which have accrued to poor clients. Piper and Marbury's experiment demonstrates that private firms involved in legal services can achieve quality results which might not otherwise be possible.

The Lawyers: Women's Rights

"If particular care and attention are not paid to the ladies," said Abigail Adams to her husband John in 1776, "we are determined to foment rebellion and will not hold ourselves bound to obey any laws in which we have no voice or representation." That same sentiment no doubt motivates the Women's Law Fund, Inc., whose principal goal is the elimination of sex discrimination.

The Fund was founded in 1972 by attorneys Jane M. Picker and Lizabeth A. Moody, both of whom had previously been active in a number of women's rights organizations. They knew of a demand for legal services by persons claiming sex discrimination, particularly in employment, and realized that few clients could afford to take advantage of the limited services available. Many established attorneys would hesitate to engage in such litigation, citing conflicts of interest or lack of expertise in a relatively poorly-defined area of law. Other organizations providing free legal services were already overburdened. Moreover, it became clear to the women that men were taking little interest in such cases; the fact that there was not much money to be made occasioned additional reluctance on the part of many established attorneys.

With seed money from the Ford Foundation and the Cleveland Foundation, the Women's Law Fund was established. Its articles of incorporation permit the Fund to furnish legal services for cases involving sex discrimination. The terms of the Ford grant limit the Foundation's funds to cases involving employment, education, housing, and government benefits. Since opening its doors, the

Women's Law Fund has become involved in a number of test cases, including determination of whether a woman is entitled to use sickness and disability leave for maternity purposes, whether a woman can be forced to take a mandatory leave of absence if she is pregnant, and whether women should be accepted for training in jobs that are traditionally male-dominated.

The general attitude of law firms has been that part-time lawyers could be employed only in research. This has been a particular problem for women attorneys who frequently divide time between child-rearing and law practice. Fund trustees feel that by working in a team, with a small amount of overlap, two part-time lawyers should be as versatile as one full-time attorney. The Fund also makes use of consultants in areas of specialization. There are now as many men around the office of the Women's Law Fund as there are women.

The Fund's activity is centered in Ohio, but aid will be given to persons in other areas of the country where key discrimination issues are involved and legal services are not otherwise available. Services are also offered to other lawyers who handle sex discrimination cases but who lack the necessary expertise.

The Women's Law Fund is the only firm engaged primarily in litigation of this kind, and as such is being watched closely. Its success will determine the future of similar organizations in other areas of the country. Helping to point the women in the right direction at this early stage in the Fund's history are a system which allows them freedom to pursue a wide spectrum of cases that will set legal precedents in the area of equal rights, a good relationship with the media, and a sincere commitment to the cause. Says one staff member: "It's not just women's rights we're fighting for. It's everybody's rights."

The National Newspaper

On the morning of October 10, 1972, Richard Nixon and other readers of *The Washington Post* may have been somewhat stunned by the paper's lead story, which began: "FBI agents have established that the Watergate bugging incident stemmed from a massive campaign of political spying and sabotage conducted on behalf of President Nixon's re-election and directed by officials of the White House and the Committee to Re-Elect the President."

The article had culminated more than three months of exhaustively intense, frequently frustrating investigative journalism by two young *Post* reporters, Carl Bernstein and Bob Woodward. Their research had been carried out in strict secrecy, but with the full support of the *Post*'s owner (Katharine Graham) and executive editor (Ben Bradlee), both of whom were being subjected to some of the most severe criticism ever leveled publicly at the press by officials of the federal government. Vice President Agnew's hottest rhetoric had been aimed in the general direction of all eastern liberal newspapers, but the Nixon Administration, rankled no end by the *Post*'s persistent sniping, singled out the Washington paper for special treatment. Attorney General John Mitchell told a reporter, "Katie Graham is going to get her tit caught in a big fat wringer," and Press Secretary Ronald Ziegler accused the *Post* of "shabby journalism" and "character assassination." Apart from the relatively harmless verbal abuse, the government challenged license renewals of the Post Company's two Florida television stations (legal fees

could reach half a million dollars). While the *Post* veri-
fied its facts on the Watergate story, its stock plummeted
fifteen points.

Mrs. Graham says she never considered halting the
Post's Watergate coverage, but she did admit to some
apprehension at the relative force of the government's criticism in comparison with earlier clashes. "The antagon-
ism between this Administration and the press was much
stronger—the degree of animosity, of real hatred. I would
say in our case that if they could have destroyed us, they
would have. Even we were not aware of the extent to
which some of the people would go to try to wipe out their
opponents. One of the worries that I had was that we might
be overplaying the story—with hindsight I would say we
were underplaying it—these people were pretty ruthless,
but I think they would have had to change the rules of
the game to get at us.

"Nevertheless, I got a feeling that there was a *High Noon*
situation developing, that this really was for keeps, that
this was the toughest thing we had ever faced, by far
tougher than publishing the Pentagon Papers. We asked
ourselves if there was some enormous Kafka plot, if we
were being led down a road to discredit the paper. The reputation of the *Post* was totally at stake."

Actually, there were a great many people besides Mrs.
Graham who thought that if the *Post* was wrong about
Watergate, Richard Nixon could have been right about
American journalism.

But by March 1973, when the President finally conceded
that political corruption in his campaign involved something more than pranks and capers, the *Post* was receiving apologies from a chagrined and chastened Ziegler and
Agnew, and acclaim for its dogged reporters and editors.
As Watergate broke, there were weeks and months when

reporters at *The New York Times* could do little but sit around waiting for the first edition of the *Post* before filing their stories, which became front-page leads.

Besides vindication of effort, however, Watergate was but a natural product of the *Post*'s stridently independent editorial policies—most of which had been sown years earlier. Mrs. Graham's father, Eugene Meyer, had bought the paper at a bankruptcy auction in 1933, when it had a circulation of about 50,000 and operated out of a falling-down building. ("He was a banker and in his late fifties, but he had always had this hankering, a real feeling that we all owe a certain amount of public service.") There were five papers in Washington at the time, the *Star* leading the pack; Meyer lost about a million dollars of his own money on the *Post*. Katharine herself worked first as a reporter in San Francisco, then returned to Washington, where she met her husband. When Philip Graham joined the paper in 1946 he was thirty years old; six months later, his father-in-law became president of the World Bank and Graham assumed the role of publisher.

Then the *Times Herald* merged with the *Post* and the new product quickly became financially solvent. In 1963, after Philip Graham's death, his wife took the reins and began to mold a new team. "You build up a feeling of what you're about. Although he was a Republican, my father had founded the paper to be an independent commentator. At the same time it was also established that the paper should do as much good news reporting as it could, but it's very expensive to do good news reporting. It takes a lot of training and skill. We couldn't just say, 'Now we are going to be a good paper.' It really does evolve."

By the time Bradlee came over as assistant managing editor in 1965, "we had a commitment," says Katharine Graham, "toward a sort of undefined excellence. A lot of people say, 'Do you want to be with *The New York Times*?

What are your ambitions?' This is a very different kind
of newspaper from *The New York Times*. We can't be the
journal of records that they are, or do the extent of the
reporting they do. But being in Washington, we can do
very interesting things with intellect and high class, and
we have a broad base—a lot of things that appeal to people.
We do heavy local reporting, which I think is very important, because a newspaper's duty is to the community. We
have the opportunity and money and staff to be a first-
rate national and international publication. We try to tell
people what is going on, what it means, and make it
understandable."

That's what the *Post* was concentrating on when the
dam broke in 1972. "Watergate was a very fine piece of
investigative work, but obviously it was of the most spec-
tacular kind because of its subject. We don't say anything
about a dozen other pieces of investigative reporting that
in their way were very good. Investigative reporting is just
incredibly difficult. People have been asking, 'Was there
one dramatic moment, one cosmic decision?' But we would
have done it no matter what Administration had been in
power; they wanted to undermine our motives, but in fact
the story was very carefully done. We were reporting on
such a sensitive area, the credibility of the government. We
always have to be careful in investigative reporting, but we
were doubly careful here. No story was printed on an anonymous source; we always had two or three. A lot of them
were Republican sources.

"When we were sure of our facts, we were in no way
going to be intimidated by a lot of noise. It bothered me
that the *Post* stood out so clearly, because I thought if it
was such a helluva big story, where are the other papers?
There were some bad moments when we had this exclusively—we had to ask ourselves, what's wrong?—I thought
that maybe we had gotten a little too exclusive. The fact is

that the sources became our sources, and then even later, when the other papers did get into it, it was really hard for them to find the sources."

Perhaps the most attractive quality that the *Post* brings to American journalism is its penchant for innovation, and one of its most important new creations has been establishment of an internal ombudsman. The current occupant of that position is Robert C. Maynard, an articulate black man who climbed the ranks without benefit of a formal college education. For a long time American journalism rested beneath the umbrella of the First Amendment and fought most criticism as an attack on freedom of speech. As the power of the media grew, however, so were their policies and practices more carefully scrutinized. Says Maynard: "The idea was that newspapers come to terms with some of the criticism being leveled at them, such as that by Agnew. But he simply crystallized what a lot of people in and out of the newspaper business felt. There was something about the nature of the press, the power it was accumulating as a result of its monopoly characteristics. Some people have said maybe a dozen basic entities determine most of what the American people are going to learn about any given event—the two wire services, the three networks, a few newspapers, *Newsweek* and *Time*. That is an oversimplification but it contains a certain truth in that there are only a few powerful voices, and if they choose to make an issue important, chances are it's going to be important—Watergate being a classical example."

The second person to hold the job on the *Post* was Ben Bagdikian. When he stepped down in August 1972, Bradlee approached Maynard. Maynard first developed his own conception of how the *Post*'s ombudsman should function in his letter to Bradlee accepting the position:

The average reader picks up *The Washington Post* to see what is new and different, while the Ombudsman picks it up to see what is right and wrong. He is to read for consistency or the lack of consistency, for fairness or the lack of fairness, for graceful language or graceless language. When he reads of how many Republican members of the House opposed the President on a given measure, he wants to know how many members of his party support the President without searching out the roll call in agate type. When he reads of an urban phenomenon, he has the duty of asking whether its suburban counterpart should also be reported. When the Ombudsman reads a description of the Sinai question written from Tel Aviv, he must wonder how fair a shake Cairo received. When he reads a sentence beginning, "He made reference also to one White House memo . . ." the Ombudsman wants to know why "He also referred to a White House memo . . ." would not have been better language.

He is the public monitor of the quality of information people receive. As such, his findings ought to form the basis for a column that appears in the newspaper no less than every 10 days. Others on the staff would write about the business as well, but an Ombudsman whose examinations don't surface regularly in print, is not an Ombudsman, but a title, a gimmick. For this reason, Phil Geyelin and Meg Greenfield should be full parties to any agreement we attempt to reach.

Not all of the columns should ponder the life-and-death questions of existence on the planet. They should be enticing invitations to our readers to share in some observations on how our business is done. When a man goes on trial for pandering and the evidence all sounds as if it came out of *Pimp*, the street novel by "Iceberg Slim," the Ombudsman might write a column about whether we were covering a trial or reporting on a phenomenon that might be called, "the bizarre world where prostitutes and their pimps live." The testimony by Sandra Mitchell against Godfrey Sterling and the Government's case against Sterling were so classically "Iceberg" that it is clear to me that we should have followed up that trial with some attempt to tell our readers how atypical Sterling's operation was, if at all. Every detail I read of the Government case would have been like *déjà vu* to a reader of *Pimp*.

About a column in four ought to be devoted to the usage of the language in the newspaper, reminding people that we don't always keep our tenses straight; that headlines have to label the central idea in a story, as well as fit the column count; that when we report on people whose discipline involves specialized terminology, we should be careful to leave the special language in the courtroom or the laboratory and tell our readers what happened in the same English they speak.

Not everything the Ombudsman observes must be made public. For one thing, that would become boring soon enough. Moreover, there is a class of housekeeping problems that I would hope could be simply solved by calling them to the Editor's attention. These would be in the area of how we are doing our job from a technical viewpoint. When jagged holes are appearing in the copy, the Ombudsman would try to discern whether the problem had a pattern that warranted further attention. If he observes a number of linguistically and stylistically ragged headlines, he might want to suggest that the Editor or Managing Editor ask the slotmen to tighten up on their troops. If he sees a headsheet and a Style piece that overtrack, he might suggest a reminder to senior editors to communicate more about the news flow. From time to time, when he sees stories based on numbers, he might run them through his calculator to see if they really add up.

Frequently, when numbers don't add up, people complain. The Ombudsman cannot do the serious job of monitoring the paper if he becomes the clearinghouse for all of the bitches and gripes of all segments of the public. A means must be devised for him to be informed about complaints, but his attention should be required only when they cannot be resolved on the desk alleged to be responsible. In short, they ought to be disputes of substance, and the Ombudsman should be the source of last

review before the matter reaches the Editor or the Managing Editor.

How the staff and the public view the Ombudsman is
crucial to the success of his mission. He must be understood from the onset to be an independent voice on the
subject of the quality of the information reaching the
public. It must be understood from the start that he does
not sit in judgment of his colleagues as individuals but
rather of their collective effort. And, to be fair, he
doesn't judge just his own colleagues' efforts, but those
of all who seek to inform the public.

It ought to be understood that his opinion, finally, is
his own and that members of the reporting and editorial
page staff are free to differ with him, and are most likely
to do so. His role has nothing to do with the day-to-day
decision-making about the operation of the newspaper.
His, necessarily, is a voice apart, even while being from
within.

As it has developed, Maynard says, the first function of the
Post's ombudsman is that of receiving any complaint by
any member of the public about anything concerning this
institution—about editorial or grammatical lapses, failure
of a newsboy to get the paper on the doorstep on time, a
bill from the accounting department that is wrong, a whole
range of complaints and concerns.

Phase two is to circulate to the various editors and
whomever, orally or in writing, Maynard's own observations about the deficiencies of the paper.

And phase three is the column, "The News Business,"
which is an attempt to discuss the problems of the practice
of journalism from a variety of areas—not just what the
Post does, but also CBS, the wires, or what they all do in
concert on any given story or what they all fail to do.

Since the time of his appointment, Maynard has written impressively candid columns in which he monitors
news and editorial operations, and offers his own views
on the performance of the media in general and of the Post

in particular. Among his concerns have been a number of in-house stories, including:

—Proof of the accuracy with which the press quoted John Ehrlichman, refuting Ehrlichman's claim that he had been misquoted.

—Questionable word choice in a headline, and the editorial judgment exercised in the placement and coverage of particular stories.

—The dearth of black characters in *Post*-carried comics, spelling errors, and rationale behind the choice of letters to the editor.

—The printing of statements attributed to anonymous sources.

Another liberal policy adopted by the *Post* has been a program of sabbatical leaves for seasoned reporters. Maynard, in fact, was on leave when offered the ombudsman's position.

"The *Post* was just beginning to formalize a sabbatical program at that time, but I had already chosen to take one beforehand. I just asked for a year off without pay. I had saved up some money and I had some friends who had this extraordinary mountaintop in northern California, about a hundred miles above San Francisco; they were planning to travel for a year and wanted somebody to look after their house. It worked out perfectly. I just took a year to myself, to pull some thoughts together (mostly dismiss some) and look at some problems in a pressure-free environment. The years from 1966 to 1971 were hell for a journalist in this country, especially a black journalist. Urban rebellion, campus rebellion, bombing demonstrations of every kind, a lot of fine folks getting hurt or killed."

Most large newspapers have a distinctive editorial and political bias and all struggle to achieve objectivity—the

Post is no exception. But when it comes to sincere and thoughtful self-scrutiny, and persistence in seeking the heart of an important story, the *Post* leaves most of its big-city competition far behind.

The Ethnic Broadcasters

"Old myths die stubbornly," says Bill Moyers in *Listening to America*, "and the myth of the melting pot—the boiling caldron pouring forth its uniform ingots of assimilated Americans—is no exception. The concept that 'All men are created equal' has often been interpreted to mean that to be different is to be un-American. . . . I remember once hearing the elders at my church—and this was in the early fifties—discuss whether 'real Americans' would be separated in heaven from 'foreign Americans.' They never resolved the issue, but the idea persisted: to be a 'good American' one should be as much like everyone else as possible."

The various mass media in America are controlled by a predominantly white, English-speaking culture. Consequently, hundreds of thousands of citizens who speak little if any English are completely cut off from access to information, news, major sources of recreation and education, a forum for discussing public issues, and a means of cultural identification. Racial and ethnic minorities operate none of the nation's 224 commercial television facilities, and fewer than 50 of the 8000 radio outlets. While larger stations may donate air time for minority-group programing, their efforts are usually limited in scope and impact.

Sonoma County, California, is situated a hundred miles north of San Francisco. Approximately 20,000 of its 205,-000 residents are Chicanos—many of them farm workers who speak no English. There are four radio stations in the area (three AM and one FM) and one television channel—all controlled by local Anglo interests—and the two and a half hours per week they provide for Mexican-American programing falls far short of meeting the needs of the Spanish-speaking population. In 1971, a group of Chicano students at Sonoma State College gathered to discuss the communications gap in their community, and developed the idea of a bilingual, bicultural radio station. They decided that to purchase an existing facility was financially prohibitive, but to build a new station was a feasible possibility. Thus was formed the Bilingual Broadcasting Foundation, Inc.

Created as a nonprofit, tax-exempt organization to run an educational FM station, Bilingual Broadcasting provides standard and experimental music, public-interest reports, and news/educational programing in both Spanish and English. There are numerous offerings beyond the more traditional formats, including series on:

—Cultural heroes (developed and presented by Chicano students).

—Modern trends in prenatal and postnatal health care, the availability of medical services, and low-cost nutritional practices.

—Legal services, in which Spanish-speaking lawyers inform the community, especially young people, of their rights and responsibilities.

—How and why to become involved in local government and public-service agencies.

The moving force behind Bilingual Broadcasting and its current director is a young Chicano named Guido Del Prado. Born in South America, he has a master's degree in psychology from Sonoma State, and at various times has been a pilot, construction worker, community organizer, and counselor. Though he and his associates started with nothing but an idea, they quickly mustered support: a

$65,000 grant from the Campaign for Human Development, a transfer by the Department of Health, Education, and Welfare of 4.9 acres of land on a defunct naval base, and numerous contributions from small foundations, businesses, and citizens. "But the commitment and perseverance of the people involved in this project," says Del Prado, "has been the most amazing factor in its success." Neither he nor his colleagues had any prior broadcasting experience. Starting literally from scratch, they studied basic studio design and engineering and devised program formats in both Spanish and English. They fenced off a barren field in open farm country outside Santa Rosa and, with little help from professional contractors, constructed a makeshift but sturdy six-room building, which has in it three studios, two offices, a lounge, and no air-conditioning. Total cost: around $12,000. The necessary licenses were acquired—not without foot-dragging from some federal agencies—and student personnel were hired and trained.

Even now, though Bilingual Broadcasting's potential listening audience is close to a half-million, its chief engineer—for want of the necessary connecting equipment—must travel a long distance each day in order to take readings at a remote transmitter. News programs must consist of clippings from newspapers and magazines, since the station has no wire-service ticker. And though enthusiasm remains strong and listener response encouraging, the station's financial status will remain uncertain as long as it is forced to rely on primary support from foundations. Plans are in the offing for production and sale of bilingual programs to other outlets around the country, lending some hope that Bilingual Broadcasting will someday become a self-sufficient enterprise.

Del Prado emphasizes that his operation is not just a radio station, but a cultural and communications center for all Spanish-speaking people within wave range.

"Let's say a teacher begins his class with: 'Okay, children. Today we are going to talk about breakfast. Look at this chart.' He shows them a picture of a tall glass of orange juice, some pancakes, some Kellogg's K-9, so on and so forth. Now that's relevant today to the English-speaking children. But the Chicano children who sit there wonder about the things they eat at home—whether it's beans, tortillas, *nopales, huevos rancheros, chorizos con huevos* —they wonder if they are eating the right things. Even though such things might be equal in nutritive value or richer, the kids don't know. Let me give you another example. The kids have to identify with someone. Like you hear many black kids say: 'I like to be like Willie Mays who swings that thing and hits the ball so beautifully and makes a lot of money.' Now I think that it's fair for the Spanish-speaking children to have professors to identify with and say: 'I'd like to be like Mr. Martínez when I grow up.' But this doesn't exist. Many times parents cannot communicate with their school system. They don't participate in community affairs, they don't belong to any PTAs, all because of the lack of language. The school administration is not doing anything at all about it."

Although certain militant elements of the Mexican-American Anti-Defamation League dislike the fact that Bilingual Broadcasting exists on "Anglo funds," they cannot deny that the small Santa Rosa station has developed a greater sense of self-understanding, self-awareness, and self-respect among the Chicanos themselves, and reversed an attitude of unconcern and even amusement in the surrounding English-speaking community. In the process, Sonoma County has acquired a strong new forum for effective citizenship.

The Media Problem-Solvers

In Chicago a bereaved, newly widowed father of a large family had immediate need for formula to feed his three-week-old baby. He took the baby to the welfare office; after waiting in line, he was refused help. From the lobby of the building, he telephoned Call For Action. Almost immediately, help was on its way: food was provided for the infant within ten minutes, and the machinery was set in motion for additional assistance for the family.

A nation-wide complaint mechanism serving a deep and growing need in urban life is one response to the nation's growing cynicism about an individual's ability to assert any meaningful influence in his community. Call For Action was established at radio station WMCA in New York City in 1963 by Ellen and Peter Straus, to receive the complaints and grievances of the ordinary citizen. Today, it is a network in 45 cities, and Call For Action's volunteer professionals answer telephone calls from people with problems of all kinds—ranging from housing and consumer fraud (the most frequent grievances) to difficulties with employment, schools, police, drugs, discrimination, and welfare. Respondents may voice complaints against individual merchants or have problems with city agencies, but all have one thing in common: they need help—and they know they will get it at Call For Action.

It takes courage on the part of broadcast management to run the risk of offending a would-be advertiser in order to share a little of the power with the people; it also takes commitment and stamina from the volunteers, who continually fight an uphill battle. But the partnership between a commercial broadcast facility and a volunteer staff provides an effective grievance mechanism.

When a municipal department or an agency to which referral was made does not respond within a reasonable time, a volunteer acts as ombudsman on behalf of the caller. The technique is direct follow-up. If necessary, the station airs editorials and documented reports. It is these broadcasts of specific abuses and community needs, asking for immediate response, that furnish the real power for Call For Action.

A blind woman, refused entrance to a San Diego restaurant because of her Seeing Eye dog, telephoned Call For Action. The volunteer checked the law and advised the station's news department of the incident; the woman was then interviewed on television. As a result, the restaurant owner publicly apologized, and he advised other restaurant owners that the law allows Seeing Eye dogs in restaurants and all public buildings.

Call For Action is distinguished from other help lines because the emphasis is on calling people back to see if help was obtained; in other services the objective is selection of the several cases which will be solved on the air or in print. In each city along the network, the project is maintained by a broadcast station which has a written agreement with Call For Action, Inc. The broadcaster provides telephones, office space, and supplies, and airs a minimum of five promotional spots daily with successful case histories—inviting listeners to call a specific number during announced hours with their own problems and complaints. All service to callers is confidential and free. Call For Action's volunteer professionals are dedicated and meticulous, following each case to conclusion. Surveys by local stations consistently indicate that 72 per cent of the people who call have their problems solved successfully.

The model project is the WMCA Call For Action in

New York City, where five days weekly, from 10 a.m. to
1 p.m., regularly scheduled volunteer professionals answer
the telephone with competence and compassion and direct
callers to the services they need. The program's social
impact goes well beyond the tens of thousands of individual grievances that it undertakes to redress. In New York,
Call For Action has moved City Hall to create a prob-
lem-referral service, improved the quality of local government by publicizing waste and inefficiency, and reinforced
in people the habit of making grievances known—with the
expectation that just complaints will be resolved. In addition, WMCA has caused the city to revise its building-code-
enforcement procedures and exposed an illegal slumlord
syndicate with information that led to four federal jury
indictments.

Although Call For Action has been criticized as a Band-
Aid approach to solving profound urban problems, it is
fast becoming a national organization where citizens can
make their voices heard. Ellen Straus is quick to point out
the difference between Call For Action and referral agencies: "We use volunteer professionals—people who are
hired, fired, trained, and supervised—to get *action*. The
least important part of their work is referral. The big thing
that distinguishes us is that we call every person back—
five, ten, fifteen times—and say, 'Did you get your electricity back on?' If not, we step in and publicly demand
that people get the services they deserve."

Though Call For Action sounds simple, most of the time
it is hard work that often becomes confusing and frustrating. But the rate of success makes all the work worth-
while. When people have been helped, there is an assurance
that somebody cares, a new faith is restored—in people,
and in the future.

"Call For Action helps citizens of the cities not only
survive but prevail," said John V. Lindsay, former Mayor

of New York City. John W. Gardner, Chairman of Common Cause, goes a bit further: "Call For Action is an ingenious means of re-establishing a link of communication between the citizen—no matter how powerless—and the systems that dominate his life. In Call For Action, the microphone and the telephone combine forces to provide an ombudsman service to our cities and to the individual citizens."

The Advertising Watchers

In August 1971 the Stern Community Law Firm, a group of Washington, D.C., attorneys specializing in media access, opened a public-interest communications center in Los Angeles under the corporate name Public Communication, Inc. The firm set out to increase the amount, type, and diversity of information offered through the mass media. A similar group, Public Interest Communications, Inc. later began operating in San Francisco.

The average television set in America is on seven hours a day. Children spend more time watching television before entering the first grade than they will spend in college classrooms for four years. The typical American viewer sees some 1400 commercials per week. Preschool children have acquired attention spans that conform to the fifteen-minute commercial break.

All of those concerned realized that nowadays, unless information is disseminated by way of the mass media, the public remains generally unaware of its existence. But the media are often closed to certain kinds of information. National networks, for example, frequently refuse to broadcast certain controversial programs; they sometimes censor conversations on talk shows and edit speeches they contend are too political. Public organizations have been refused air time and newsmen have been fired for discussing controversial subjects.

When faced with these facts, even citizens who do not shock easily sit up and take notice. Both Public Communication, Inc., and Public Interest Communications, Inc. seek to dismantle these barriers. The Stern group operates on the premise "that techniques of media access of publicity, when coupled with legal advice and litigation, can effectively direct public attention to social problems, provide consumers with information to act in their own self-interests, and focus the pressure of public scrutiny on the courts, administrative agencies, and other decision-making bodies." This premise is based on three assumptions. First, public-interest groups lack the skills and the means to convey *their* information to the public. "It does not do much good to write a million nice articles when all the people are watching television," says Tracy Westen, head of the Los Angeles office. Second, if given the opportunity, entertainers, artists, photographers, graphic designers, producers, and other professionals in the communications industry—currently stifled from applying their expertise to social problems—will contribute their skills to disseminate important public information. And third, a public-interest communications firm cannot function without the continuing participation of experienced media attorneys: legal skills are required to document social abuse, research and define minority rights, screen out deceptively worded or potentially libelous advertisements, avoid pitfalls under the Internal Revenue laws, and conduct litigation against censorship of controversial, important public messages. Public Communication, Inc., thus coordinates the efforts of public-interest research organizations, lawyers, and communications artists, combining their expertise to produce social change more quickly and efficiently.

Public Interest Communications is a nonprofit resource center that provides complete advertising, media, design, and public-relations services either free of charge or at greatly reduced rates to a broad-based national constituency of issue-oriented groups. These include environmentalists, minority and prisoner organizations, community associations, women's groups, consumer-protection agencies, public-interest law firms, and many others. PIC uses the techniques of professional advertising in order to do the job most effectively.

In the past it has produced national advertising campaigns for newspapers, magazines, television, and radio. Sometimes, client groups pay to get these ads in the media, but often, especially in the case of radio and television spots, PIC attempts to secure free time and space for issue-oriented public-service ads. In addition to producing effective materials, much of PIC's work involves developing organizing techniques to broaden citizen access to the media.

PIC was formed by a number of people who had experience in both political organizing and professional advertising, and who, like Public Communication, Inc., felt that media systems in this country, while they are perhaps the most developed in the world, have offered very little chance for advocacy groups to present their positions in their own terms with anything like the sophistication of technique available to those who sell soap or automobiles. Both PIC and PCI feel that the public-service campaigns run by industry groups such as the Advertising Council are generally insufficient. PIC is also engaged in building a resource bank of professionals in the advertising business who can be called upon to contribute skills to specific campaigns.

Supported by grants from foundations and individuals (clients generally pay production costs), PIC devotes about 50 per cent of its work to local groups in its home city of San Francisco. Public-service television and radio spots, press conferences, design of brochures, posters, and leaflets are all produced by PIC's community workshop, which has been successful in raising local money to support its work. (This local aspect of PIC work could usefully and easily be replicated by similar communications centers in every major city in the country.)

Public Communication, Inc. has achieved much to its credit in a very short time. Its efforts at "countercommercials" derive from continued exploration of the "Fairness Doctrine," a policy established by the Federal Communications Commission which requires broadcasters to assure balanced treatment of controversial subjects by providing air time for opposing points of view. When the Federal Trade Commission proposed "counter-advertising" as one means of implementing the doctrine, the broadcasting industry dismissed it as "nonsense"—if stations were to provide time for groups or individuals to attack sponsors, they said, advertisers would abandon television. Public Communication, Inc., forcefully argues that counter-advertising makes commercial interests *more* responsive to the public welfare and, indeed, substantially improves their products.

In 1971 PCI's creative center began producing the first consumer-service advertisements for television. Using the donated talents of actors, musicians, and film technicians, they created five television messages: two urging owners of nearly seven million Chevrolets to have their dangerously defective engine mounts repaired; another reporting the American Medical Association's conclusion that plain, inexpensive aspirin is preferable to Excedrin, Anacin, Bufferin, and other mixtures, and recommending that viewers buy the least expensive aspirin that it could find. All three of these spots were narrated by Burt Lancaster. Carroll O'Connor appears on the screen to describe an 1899 federal law which offers citizens a reward for reporting incidents of water pollution. A fifth message, written and presented by Robert Lamm and "Chicago," warned against hard-drug abuse. Each announcement was produced for less than $1000 (a typical commercially produced ad costs about $20,000). Background documentation—supplied by groups like the Center for Auto Safety, the Medical Committee for Human Rights, and the Natural Resources Defense Council—assured factual accuracy.

Since then, the PCI has branched out to other media—print advertisements and radio messages—in its effort effectively to provide Americans with vital consumer, safety, and legal information. The creative center has also been involved in distributing voter-registration information in national magazines and in millions of record albums, encouraging musical groups to produce radio and television announcements on important legal and social issues, stimulating entertainment figures to fund the efforts of public-interest organizations, and forming liaisons with writers, actors, announcers, and production crews for future work. Over 300 radio stations in the top 100 markets now broadcast countercommercials on a regular basis throughout their weekly programing as a free public service.

Meanwhile, PCI has dovetailed its litigation with the creative center's projects, seeking to reduce "censorship" over free-speech messages by privately owned radio and television programs. The firm has argued for free access to the mass media by consumer-oriented public-service groups and by Congressmen, in favor of paid access for Congressional programing and editorial messages, and for application of the Fairness Doctrine to cases involving various commercial interests and minority political parties. It has fought against direct station censorship of television "talk shows" and against political pressures on programing content.

Says Tracy Westen: "What we are working for is free speech—but *really* free speech. As long as you have a system of paid speech it means that people without money don't get to say anything, and that has got to be changed. Under the Sixth Amendment the law is that if you don't have any money, you can get a lawyer free of charge. Our argument is that the First Amendment is just as important as the Sixth."

The Local Newspapers

Editor and publisher Barry Bingham, Jr., invokes the heritage passed along by his father and grandfather: "You have got to show courage in your editorial columns." The Louisville *Courier-Journal* and the *Louisville Times* have always pointedly concentrated on two basic functions of the press: broad, comprehensive news coverage and a vigorous editorial policy.

Perhaps largely because of a commitment by the papers' ownership toward full racial equality, Louisville has been a step ahead of many other Southern communities in putting an end to segregation in schools, swimming pools, and other public facilities. Pollution control and soil conservation also receive strong editorial support. As far back as the 1930s the paper backed family-planning education, and now favors the recent Supreme Court decision on abortion. The Bingham family says that its paper is "independent" and supports the "best" candidate, whether Republican or Democrat.

Another important aspect of editorial policy is the liberal publication of correspondence. Virtually all "Letters to the Editor" are printed—many of course expressing disagreement (ranging from dismay to outrage) with earlier editorials. In response to charges of bias, the paper has begun a column called "Letters *from* the Editors," which explains their job and how they perceive it.

Comprehensive local news coverage is an example of the dedication to being responsive to *all* the citizens of Kentucky and the Louisville metropolitan area. Every day, four separate editions of the morning *Courier-Journal* are pulled off the press. The first goes to the far reaches of the state, the next to areas somewhat closer to home, the third edition to the readership in Indiana, and the latest for Louisville itself. The *Courier-Journal* maintains several permanent offices in various towns around the state in order to insure full coverage of local events. Such widespread news-gathering makes the *Courier-Journal* a truly regional paper.

But the *Courier-Journal* is perhaps most noteworthy for its implementation of several innovative practices that have been subsequently adopted by other papers throughout the country. In 1967, Bingham appointed the company's own ombudsman—the first on any American newspaper. The effects were immediately noticeable. As of mid-1973, some 12,000 complaints had been handled, including those from a governor, several mayors, county judges, and school-board members. Most of the calls and letters have been from average citizens who felt that there had been a mistake in the paper's coverage of particular facts. In some cases, the follow-up stories are written to clarify the news as first reported; in others, errors are simply admitted. The *Courier-Journal* and *Louisville Times* were among the first newspapers in the nation to display their failures in a prominent editorial position (the *Courier* under the heading "Beg Your Pardon," the *Times* under "We Were Wrong"). A daily report of comments from readers, and the answers they are given, goes to various executives and editors. Copies sent to the city editors are made available to their news staffs, so everyone from cub reporters on up may know what the readers are thinking.

Another first instituted by both the *Courier-Journal* and *Louisville Times* is the position of advertising ombudsman, whose job (since April 1972) has been to review the more than 6000 advertisements which appear each day, and to prevent fraudulent, misleading, or deceptive claims from appearing in print. The advertising ombudsman also determines whether an ad may be considered effective or in bad taste. To date, he has censored more than $100,000 in potential ad revenue. (In particular, national-health-insurance advertisements must follow rigid guidelines before acceptance, as do other such "products.") All advertising accepted by the *Courier-Journal* and *Louisville Times* is published on the premise that the merchandise and services offered are accurately described and willingly sold to customers at the advertised price. Advertisers are made aware of these conditions in advance. Ads that are deceptive or misleading are never knowingly accepted. Readers are encouraged to report noncompliance with these standards.

The *Courier-Journal* was also one of the first newspapers in the country to employ a six-column format, designed for readability. It is still one of the few papers to carry continuations of front-page stories on the back page of the first section (losing fewer readers than were they run over to inside pages).

Although located in the country's thirty-ninth largest city, the *Courier-Journal* is consistently recognized by its peers as among the top ten newspapers in the United States. A recent independent survey placed the *Courier-Journal* third—behind *The New York Times* and *The Los Angeles Times*—among all daily American papers on the basis of journalistic quality, impartial news reporting, and action in the public welfare. Another sampling (by *Seminar* Magazine) named the *Courier-Journal* the third "most fair" newspaper in the United States. (*The Christian Science Monitor* and *The Wall Street Journal* were in first and second place in that category.) And in 1961, the *Courier-Journal* and the *Louisville Times* were rated by the nation's journalism profession as the best pair of newspapers, morning and evening, published by the same organization.

In addition, staff members have been honored five times with the Pulitzer Prize, the newspaper industry's highest award for journalistic excellence. (The first went to Henry Watterson for two World War I editorials. The second was to *Courier-Journal* reporter "Skeets" Miller for his coverage of the Floyd Collins cave tragedy in 1922. The third was awarded to *Louisville Times* cartoonist Robert York for a cartoon on the precarious farm-price situation in 1955. The fourth was won by the *Courier-Journal* in 1967 for "meritorious public service" in its fight against the ravages of strip-mining. The most recent Pulitzer Prize went to staff writer John Fetterman in 1968 for coverage of the funeral of a Vietnam casualty from Kentucky.)

The newspapers have also won numerous awards for make-up, typography, reporting, and public service. The *Courier-Journal*, the *Louisville Times*, and the Sunday *Magazine* have frequently been cited for photographic excellence. The *Courier-Journal* has been named five times in the last nine years as the U.S. newspaper that makes the best use of photographs. (The award was in the Pictures of the Year competition conducted by the National Press Photographers Association and the University of Missouri School of Journalism.)

The Binghams would never consider owning a newspaper in another city, although they have been approached on numerous occasions. "We know Louisville, we are dedicated to this community, and we could never feel that way about a city where we don't live." The *Courier-Journal* has been around since 1868 and the *Louisville Times*, its afternoon associate, since 1884. In 1918, Judge Robert Worth Bingham bought controlling interest in the company and became editor of the *Courier-Journal*, in the process forming the family-owned corporation which exists today. Judge Bingham was a philanthropic man, who held the newspapers as a "public trust." He remained at their helm until 1933, when he became Ambassador to the Court of St. James's. Management of the company passed first to Barry Bingham, Sr., then to his son.

The family appears to be one of the last in a dying breed, plowing a substantial part of its corporate profits into improvement of news coverage, distribution, technological innovation, and staff hiring. The *Courier-Journal* has one of the highest dollar-expenditures for news-gathering of any paper in the country. It has succeeded in attracting outstanding journalists from other high-ranking newspapers, largely because unbiased reporting is held as an absolute standard, individual enterprise is encouraged, and a strong editorial policy is pursued.

In Government

The Ombudsman

Despite the intricate constitutional safeguards afforded by a built-in system of checks and balances, separation of powers, and numerous other protections of life and liberty, there exists a noticeable gap: citizens can defend themselves against just about anyone except the government itself. The federal, state, or local bureaucracy may subject citizens to all sorts of indignities—even loss of life, limb, and property—without having to face the consequences.

Relatively seldom is a public agency or public official held legally accountable for misconduct. Beyond the inhibitions brought about by keeping the three traditional branches of government separate, other problems obtain. Judicial review is too costly, too slow, and too poorly understood to serve as an effective means of redress for personal grievances that may have little public impact or involve small sums of money. While legislators do resolve a number of individual complaints, their labors on behalf of constituents are not a wholly satisfying means for righting wrongs; though the partisan and part-time nature of most legislatures renders assistance through special treatment—a phone call or letter—it seldom brings about a basic change in administrative procedures. Internal appeals, hot lines, and volunteer agencies help to amplify the voice of the citizenry, but too often they are not intensive and thorough enough to have a lasting effect on the bureaucracy. Sorely needed is a third-party critic to make certain that complaints receive fair hearings and that proper remedies are found—a supplement to the present corrective procedures which are too often confusing, episodic, partial, selective, and frustrating.

The office of ombudsman—an individual charged with seeing that the law is not administered with an evil eye or uneven hand—was first established in Sweden in 1809, and the institution has been retained by most Scandinavian countries ever since. The ideal ombudsman, according to proponents of the idea, is a high-level officer with adequate salary and status, free and independent of both the agencies he may criticize and the power that appoints him, with a long tenure in office once appointed (sufficient to immunize him from the natural pressures of seeking reappointment), and with the power to investigate administrative practices on his own initiative. His sole job is to receive and act upon complaints without charge to the complainant. Since he does not have punitive authority, his principal weapons are publicity and persuasion, criticism and reporting.

In July 1969, Hawaii became the first state in the union to appoint an ombudsman. His office was funded by an appropriation of $103,000, and he was given wide authority to investigate the internal activities of state agencies and to intervene at any time in any administrative matter. His jurisdiction extends to all permanent government entities, departments, organizations, or institutions, and to all persons acting in the exercise of their official duties. (Exempt from the ombudsman's purview are the courts; the legislature, its committees, and staff; the federal government; multistate authorities; and the governor and his personal staff.)

Hawaii's ombudsman is appointed by a majority vote of each house of the legislature to a six-year term (with possible reappointment for two more). His independence is further protected by the requirement that no less than two-thirds of the members of each house of the legislature must vote for his removal or suspension for neglect of duty, misconduct, or disability. Thus the ombudsman may determine his own internal procedures, his staff serves at his pleasure, and neither he nor his subordinates may be required to testify in court with respect to official matters. The ombudsman's effectiveness is determined by the esteem in which he is held and public acceptance of the reasonableness of his views. In Hawaii his status is further enhanced by the fact that he is paid the same salary as circuit court judges and provided the same immunities from civil and criminal liability.

Administrative changes that have been made in the state as a result of the ombudsman's investigations:

—Inmates at the Hawaii State Prison now have the right to file grievances with prison authorities.

—The Department of Regulatory Agencies now sends a letter of explanation along with all dismissed complaints.

—Interest is paid on rental security deposits for leased space at Hawaii airports.

—The Contract License Board now requires most home-improvement contractors to enter into written agreements with consumers.

But the greatest improvements have taken place in individual cases. The aggrieved citizen in Hawaii need no longer tolerate the official runaround: he complains directly to the ombudsman by letter, phone, or personal visit, and the ombudsman's staff makes the rest of the calls. In fiscal year 1970–71 almost 2000 Islanders (a 79 per cent increase over the previous year) chose to contact their ombudsman first.

Hawaii's first and current ombudsman is Herman Doi, a lawyer and the former director of the University of Hawaii's Legislative Reference Bureau. He may investigate any complaint or administrative practice which might be contrary to law, unreasonable, unfair, oppressive, or perhaps discriminatory even though in accordance with the law. He may also look into administrative dispositions based on a mistake in facts, improper or irrelevant grounds, unaccompanied by an adequate statement of reasons, performed in an inefficient manner, or otherwise erroneous. He may examine the facts on his own motion or on behalf of a complainant, and he has the right to make inquiries, obtain information, enter without notice to inspect the premises of an agency, and hold private hearings. He has the power to subpoena both persons and records, and to seek enforcement of a $1000 penalty against any person who refuses to comply with his lawful demands.

While the ombudsman does not have power to punish maladministrators or reverse administrative decisions, he does have at his disposal substantial means for internal reporting, persuading, criticizing, and publicizing. If a negligent or misbehaving agency fails to act on his recommendations, the ombudsman may present his opinion to the governor, the legislature, and/or the public. If he feels that there has been a breach of duty or criminal misconduct, he refers the matter to the appropriate authorities. Since the ombudsman is ultimately responsible to the citizenry, he must submit to the legislature and to the public an annual report of his activities.

Hawaiians now see their complaints against government activities investigated by an independent body, without cost. Administrators are aware of a continuous review of their activities. The public has access to decision-makers, and a catalyst for the adoption of fairer and speedier rules, regulations, and laws.

"The ombudsman cannot do everything," Doi concedes. "I'm not a judge, an advocate, a legislator, nor an administrator. I am an intermediary between the people and government who strives to reduce errors, injustices, or excesses of administrators. Without a large respect for human rights, without a high regard for law, without genuine reform in government, the ombudsman would be ineffective in resolving conflct." Nevertheless, ombudsman Doi believes his office is here to stay. From all accounts his constituency would seem to agree.

The Safety Inspectors

Not all parts of the federal government are stultified bureaucracies. There are two federal agencies primarily concerned with air-transportation safety (the Federal Aviation Administration, a 55,000-people, $1.57-billion unit which oversees the operating, licensing, and administration of air transportation, and the National Transportation Safety Board, an independent body created by the Transportation Act of 1966, which reports directly to Congress), one of which does an exceptionally good job.

By federal standards the NTSB is minuscule. Charged with investigating and determining the cause of both air- and land-transportation accidents, and making recommendations to appropriate authorities in order to prevent similar mishaps in the future, its governing board is composed of five members (no more than three of whom may be of the same political party), and its staff is divided into two investigative arms: the Bureau of Aviation Safety and the Bureau of Transportation Safety. More than 80 per cent of the employees (about 150) and budget (about $6 million) is devoted to matters of aviation. The Board emphasizes its function as an information agency; it has no enforcement power other than that of persuasion. Says Charles O. Miller, Director of the Bureau of Aviation Safety: "We don't undersell this approach. As a matter of fact we are quite pleased with it. A great deal of what we do is geared to keeping the public informed. We take this responsibility quite seriously."

The work of the small and expert Accident Prevention Branch of the NTSB represents public service at its best.

It is this unit which identifies both real and potential air-transportation hazards and, based upon extensive investigation, makes recommendations for improvement. In many cases they can save lives and property. Such proposals are accorded substantial weight and credibility by public-interest groups and aviation professionals, since they are based on independent and objective appraisals of the facts.

The Accident Prevention Branch has conducted numerous special studies, providing detailed analysis of such things as:

—Jet exhausts (huge amounts of air blasted from the power plants of large planes have tossed individuals thirty feet and knocked down portions of air terminals).

—Mid-air collisions (a problem particularly serious for small aircraft).

—Air-taxi safety (upgrading regulations).

—Approach and landing accidents (perhaps the most critical and deadly aspect of air travel).

More than half of the Accident Prevention Branch's recommendations have been duly implemented—an impressive enough record, given the conscientious and rigorous approach of the agency and the fact that it is often frustrated or undermined by a federal system which sometimes appears to encourage inefficiency. Each proposed change must pass through multifarious stages, among them a comprehensive investigation leading to specific recommendations, a review by the five-person Board (usually resulting in referral to the FAA), and other reviews by separate agencies. The Aviation Administration's response is assessed for its appropriateness, compliance, and acceptability. If the Safety Board is not satisfied with the proffered plan for implementation, the process continues until agreement is reached or the matter has been rejected.

The frustration occurs when recommendations are

pointedly ignored. While the NTSB and the Accident Prevention Branch realize that any proposed change is bound to evoke disagreement, they also view the public as their clients and its safety as their primary responsibility. Those charged with implementation, on the other hand, are often closely allied with business and professional interests—making them somewhat reluctant to implement any recommendations which would result in increased costs to the air-transportation industry.

During the calendar year 1972, over 200 recommendations of varying degrees of severity were sent from the NTSB to the FAA. Each was based on careful investigation and analysis of the costs and benefits related to alternative remedial action. The record of implementation, however, speaks for itself:

—The Case of the Cessna 150 Electric Flap Actuator Malfunctions. Thirteen incidents of believed inadvertent flap retraction over a three-year period led to the recommendation that operators of single-engine aircraft with electric flaps be advised immediately of the hazard, and of appropriate techniques to assure pilot control in the event of flap system malfunction. After more than a year's delay, Cessna was required by the FAA to replace this device in all planes.

—The Case of Fuel Line Proximity to Hot Exhaust Systems. Several incidents led to recommendations that the FAA examine the fuel line/engine and exhaust incompatibility on Cessna 320s and others. Partial acceptance of this recommendation occurred three years later.

—The Case of Annual Proficiency Checks for Instrument Rated Pilots. A mid-air collision in Hendersonville, North Carolina, led to a proposal for annual pilot proficiency checks. Again, a three-year span between recommendation and implementation.

—The Case of Passive Radar Reflectors. Two mid-air collisions resulted in a recommendation that all aircraft under 12,500 pounds possess radar-passive reflectors suitable for detection up to 125–150 miles. The FAA contended that no suitable passive radar reflectors were available, but waited over a year and a half before asking their research and development department to develop such a device.

Since the NTSB's recommendations are not mandatory, acceptance and implementation are largely dependent upon other factors, such as the statutory requirement for public disclosure of all recommendations; the recording of recommendations, replies, analyses of replies; the filing of periodic progress reports to the public and Congress; and continuous follow-up action by the Accident Prevention Branch on the FAA for acceptance of its recommendations. When these procedures are challenged—as they have been by the Executive Branch, which has claimed that the recommendations reflect badly on other government agencies—the public's safety is endangered and its right to know is undermined.

The Accident Prevention Branch of the NTSB, conducting its investigations with professional sincerity, honesty, responsibility, and pride in thoroughness, thus serves as a model for other government agencies engaged in protecting and promoting the public welfare.

The Small Claims Court

A small claims court is meant to be in the truest sense the court of the people. It is here that an ordinary citizen can bring complaints involving a simple contract or tort with damages easily specified in dollars. He can collect a debt, recover the value of defective merchandise, or gain reimbursement for expenses incurred as a result of action by another party. He need not hire a lawyer. This is his local court, reflecting local circumstances and sensitive to local publicity and local pressures for reform.

Unfortunately, most small claims courts fail to achieve their potential; for the majority of consumers they are either unavailable, unusable, or invisible. (In local jurisdictions containing more than 41 million Americans, small claims courts have yet to be established.) In many areas courtroom sessions smack of so much procedural formality that representation by a lawyer is a necessity. Even where the courts are relatively effective and informal, the public remains unaware of their availability. Though intended as a means to redress individual grievances, many small claims courts have become collection agencies serving corporations and landlords. Most courts have no printed manuals which instruct citizen-litigants how to proceed. Hearings are held at inconvenient times and are unnecessarily long. Collecting a judgment from landlords or corporate defendants with high-powered legal representation is difficult if not virtually impossible.

Despite the fact that small claims courts, because they are locally run and administered and because they can provide direct and immediate benefits to consumers, present

an ideal target of citizen reform, few such improvements
take place. A glowing exception is the Harlem Small Claims
Court, in operation since January 1972.

Small claims courts were introduced in New York in
1934 as a means of dispensing justice on claims up to $50
(now up to $500) in a simplified, inexpensive way. An
important feature is that corporations, partnerships, associations, and assignees are excluded from bringing suit.
The Harlem Small Claims Court is part of the larger New
York City civil court system under the direction of Justice
Edward Thompson. Besides its location—170 West 121st
Street—the Harlem court is distinctive for its advertising, its paralegal consumer advocates, and its advice
sheets. All are the result of a joint effort by the Depart-
ment of Consumer Affairs of New York and the New York
Civil Court, with funding from the Harlem Model Cities
Program.

Although it is neither illegal nor unethical for courts
to advertise, few ever consider publicizing their services.
In Harlem such notification was essential, since the Small
Claims Court started from scratch. So consumer advocates
(in cooperation with the Office of Consumer Affairs) bom-
barded the community with literature about the court.
Posters were placed in stores, housing projects, and
schools. The Department of Consumer Affairs distributed
a step-by-step manual, "How to Sue in Small Claims Court
in N.Y.C." Local television and radio spots were produced
and broadcast.

All the advertising and publicity quickly brought citizens to the court. Once there, four paralegal advocates—
residents of the area employed by the Department of
Consumer Affairs—advise parties of their rights and show
them how to prepare cases and keep an eye open for violations of the law. In addition, they often serve as interme-
diaries between plaintiffs and potential defendants and

try to resolve disputes before they reach court, a substantial saving of time and expense.

In a community where the people have always been defendants—in landlord-tenant cases, in family court, in support actions—courts are feared places. The advocates act as the necessary bridges between the community and the court. Prior to trial they help each litigant fill out the required forms, explain what facts are needed to prove a case, and provide information about court procedures. The advocates will soon publish "Advice Sheets" on the most common cases, describing the types of evidence needed by both plaintiffs and defendants.

The advocates (and a Puerto Rican interpreter) sit in the court clerk's office, where to file a complaint costs $3 and change (refundable to the plaintiff who wins his case). Summonses are served by registered mail. Trial dates are set for two to three weeks after a complaint is filed. Court sessions are informal, and held in the evening. Cases are decided by a judge or volunteer arbitrators—lawyers with at least five years of experience. Though cases heard by arbitrators may not be appealed, community advocates are allowed in court with the plaintiff so that they may observe attorneys, arbitrators, and litigants, and note recent developments in consumer law, the need for an interpreter, or failure to understand the reasons for decision.

Sensitivity to the people and their problems is held to be paramount. Most arbitrators are blacks or Puerto Ricans who requested assignment to the Harlem court. Both arbitrators and judges are interested first in hearing and solving cases, and second with correct form and procedure. The ground rules are simple: the plaintiff speaks first (without interruption), questions are raised by the defendants, the defendant presents his case, and the plaintiff asks questions. Most cases are decided the same night; a few decisions are rendered by mail. The advocate informs a victorious plaintiff of the remedies available if a defendant has refused to pay a judgment.

In its first two years of operation the Harlem Small Claims Court tried over 4000 cases, 96 per cent of which were decided in the plaintiff's favor (to the tune of close to $700,000).

Although many small claims courts reflect in microcosm a great deal of the exploitation that shoots through American society, they also offer solutions to a great many social ills. In Harlem, justice is based on equity—a sense of how things should be—and citizens discover that justice can be direct, effective, swift, and occasionally work *for* them.

The Prison Officials

Disturbances in American prisons have focused attention on the process of criminal justice in America, and with that awareness has come greater scrutiny of federal, state, and local systems for rehabilitation and parole—by legislators, correction officials, and the public.

Inmates frequently have few alternatives after they have served their time. They may be discharged completely, paroled under supervision, sent to a prerelease center or a halfway house—or kept in prison. About 97 per cent of felons now in prison will eventually be returned to society. The majority are placed on supervised parole, bound by a set of strictly controlled regulations.

But inmates contend that they do not know what is expected from them in order to be released on parole, that they have no indication until their first parole hearing several months after incarceration, and that what they are told at the initial hearing may be changed at subsequent hearings if different board members are present. At issue are alleged denials of parole without clearly stated grounds for negative parole decisions. There have been several court responses to such grievances, and in 1971 the Supreme Court ordered the Chairman of the U.S. Board of Parole to meet with lawyers and spell out criteria for parole selection.

At the same time studies began to show that the U.S. Department of Labor programs for training prison inmates were not completely effective because rehabilitative training programs were not coordinated with release decisions of parole boards. As a consequence, a severe time lag existed between the end of rehabilitative training programs and release decisions, and it affected the desired end result of the training—employment of offenders in training-related jobs.

After some discussions, the American Correctional Association was funded to study the problem and to develop a model for prison and parole board coordination and cooperation by the Labor Department's Office of Research. Emerging from the National Workshop for Corrections and Parole Administrators (New Orleans, February 1972) was a set of guidelines which subsequently developed into a demonstration project: the Mutual Agreement Program.

Under the supervision of correctional officials an inmate's strengths and weaknesses are assessed and a personalized program of "optimal resource utilization" is formulated, designed to prepare him for successful adjustment following his release on parole. The original plan of treatment and training objectives is developed by the inmate himself. He is immediately involved in contractual negotiations with prison staff members and paroling authorities. The resulting agreement is a legally binding contract that specifies in clear terms the objectives sought in the areas of education, vocational training, discipline, and treatment, the prisoner's promise to complete them, and a definite parole date contingent upon successful completion of the agreed-upon goals.

This formal document, and the procedures surrounding its creation, are important means by which the prisoner becomes involved in—and is in fact given much of the responsibility for—his own rehabilitation and release. Prison and parole authorities are likewise brought together in closer cooperation. The Mutual Agreement Program also serves to make the prisoner feel what he should reasonably expect of himself.

Currently, three model corrections projects are in operation. The first was initiated at the Wisconsin Correctional Institution, Fox Lake; the second at the Arizona State Prison, Florence; the third at the Central City Community Center, Los Angeles. Participants in these programs include both men and women offenders, chosen on a strictly random-selection basis. At all three institutions the system is working well. Inmates and corrections officials are negotiating increasingly productive and realistic contracts and less time is being served behind bars. Both Wisconsin and Arizona officials are involved in developing plans to extend the Mutual Agreement Program to the state's other penal institutions.

The implications of Mutual Agreement Programs are significant. At the very least they create articulated criteria for parole selection and release, increase cooperation and effectiveness among participating agencies, and improve the offender's economic stability and prospects for successful participation in the community of his choice. Perhaps even more important, they shift part of the responsibility for meeting essential rehabilitative goals to the inmate—who thus obtains a measure of equality in negotiation of his contract with parole and corrections personnel, helps set long- and short-range treatment objectives for himself, and, in essence, makes himself responsible for his own rehabilitation and release.

The California Program, in addition to a contract, allows an inmate to reside at a halfway house and makes available to each participant a voucher to purchase educational and vocational training services in the community, as opposed to the use of limited prison training.

Variations on the basic concept are being tried with adult felons in Michigan prisons, with probationers in New

Jersey, and with juvenile delinquents in Virginia. The flexibility of the approach is demonstrated by the interest expressed by several other states to adapt the model to the various intervention points of the criminal-justice process.

The Consumer Protectors

The Mercantile Paradox: most businessmen are considered honest, but perhaps a majority of consumers feel themselves victimized at the marketplace. Poorly trained clerks and cashiers, small discourtesies and small deceits, computerized bill forms with uncorrected errors, frequently combined with a paucity of concern for the customer, move vendor and vendee further and further apart.

In the ocean of cynicism this often creates, however, there are islands of hope. Two of them are the Nassau County (New York) and Montgomery County (Maryland) Offices of Consumer Affairs.

In New York, some 40,000 consumers have sought help from the Nassau County OCA in the first seven years of its existence, during which time more than $800,000 in refunds and adjustments have been obtained. Nassau County was a pioneer. The first of its kind to be established at the county level, the OCA has been resolving complaints and eliminating consumer problems for local residents since 1967. It has undertaken an all-out effort not only to eliminate complaints but to resolve the problems that *cause* the complaints, putting to good use various provisions of the local law which prohibits unfair trade practices.

The Nassau County OCA remains somewhat unique in the spectrum of government-level offices protecting the consumer, although some of its more notable programs have been emulated by others around the country. These range from special in-depth investigations into unconscionable practices, to senior citizen programs, home improvement licensing, weights-and-measures testing and inspection, regulation of fuel-oil delivery, and adulteration checks of gasoline.

Certain business practices seemed so unconscionable to Nassau County consumers that they demanded prompt and intensive remedial action. The OCA conducted in-depth investigations of the retail advertising industry, health spas, unsafe toys, supermarkets, child photographers, and "cents-off specials." Such studies were engendered in different cases by large volumes of particular complaints, or by the OCA's own professional awareness of widespread problems. Following the investigations the offending parties—which have included top corporate executives—were summoned to private conferences to discuss their particular unfair trade practices. The conferences have proved highly effective in correcting consumer problems without recourse to the courts. New advertising regulations have also been promulgated which require that advertised merchandise be available for sale, comparison prices be true, free offers be explained, and prices be conspicuously displayed. Other regulations concern safety of leased equipment and harassment of debtors.

Between August and November 1971, the OCA made a thorough investigation of unsafe toys. A large number of hazardous playthings, many of which had been banned by the FDA but not removed from sale, were still being sold to unsuspecting parents. Complaints by consumers on dangerous toys were forwarded to the federal government for further investigation. As a result of this campaign the county executive recommended that the Toy Safety Act be amended to include stricter inspection and testing of all toys, domestic and imported, *prior* to their distribution to retail outlets. (Responsibility for such testing would rest with the manufacturer.) In addition, it was proposed that manufacturers and retailers be held responsible for the swift removal of all toys reported to be unsafe, and that penalties be imposed on both for failure to comply with an official recall of any unsafe product from the marketplace.

Making consumers aware of deceptive trade practices so that they can protect themselves is the principal objective of the OCA's information and education program. This is accomplished by way of releases to newspapers and magazines, radio and television, and through hundreds of speaking engagements, library exhibits, and participation in conferences and special events. The OCA also conducts an extensive program to educate grade- and high-school students about sound money-management practices.

Recognizing that older people who live on fixed incomes are hit particularly hard by inflationary prices, the OCA inaugurated a Senior Citizens Program that offers suggestions on how to handle door-to-door salesmen, as well as information about the availability of insurance, transportation costs, and day-to-day shopping techniques.

A hot line by which senior citizens may call in their complaints was installed. Groups of elderly persons throughout the county were asked to appoint spokesmen whose responsibility it will be to receive the complaints of their fellow members and forward them to the OCA for investigation. In addition, volunteers who work at the OCA, answering and expediting complaints, were enlisted and a speakers group, made up of senior citizens, was established to inform of the OCA's willingness to help and advise on particular problems. The OCA has also called upon the major supermarket chains to break up large family-sized packages of produce (e.g. five pounds of potatoes) into smaller quantities for older people.

The Consumermobile, a traveling complaint registry and information/education unit, started rolling in 1970. Almost 15,000 individuals who might otherwise not have been reached by the OCA were able to discuss their problems at the mobile, fully equipped, 32-foot trailer, manned by three community service aides and a director. The mobile unit visits schools, factories, bus terminals, community centers, neighborhood parks, and shopping centers.

The OCA was instrumental in achieving local legislation to require the licensing of all persons engaged in home-improvement businesses in Nassau County, to safeguard homeowners from deceptive practices on the part of itinerant contractors, repairmen, and remodelers. The Commissioner is authorized to refuse, suspend, or revoke a license if, after a hearing, the applicant is shown to have repeatedly failed to perform his contracts, employed untrustworthy management personnel, engaged in fraud or misrepresentation, or made false statements in his application for a license. Specifically prohibited: abandonment; willful failure to perform, without justification, any home-improvement contracts or project engaged in or undertaken; deviation from or disregard for plans or specifications in any material respect, without consent of the owner; or accepting any mortgage or promissory note or other evidence of indebtedness upon the obligations of a home-improvement transaction, with the knowledge that it entails a greater monetary obligation than the agreed consideration for the home-improvement work. Violators may be punished by revocation or suspension of their license, with fines up to $500, or by imprisonment for not more than sixty days.

The OCA's weights-and-measures inspection program includes testing and sealing of scales and other devices, commodity inspection and control, special investigations, prosecutions and fines.

Consumerism—the movement to insure bargaining parity between the business community and the buying public—has been reflected in American statutory law for more than a century, but not until recently have state enforcement agencies been formed. The Montgomery County

(Maryland) OCA was set into action in December 1971 by
an unusually strong consumer bill passed by the County
Council, which states its intent in no uncertain terms:

> to prohibit unfair, deceptive trade practices upon con-
> sumers within Montgomery County, to assist consumers
> in obtaining relief from such practices, to prevent such
> practices from occurring within Montgomery County; to
> educate consumers in trade practices involving merchan-
> dise, services and credit areas; to create an Office of Con-
> sumer Affairs to administer and assure enforcement of
> the provisions of this enactment; and to foster trade
> practices which are in the best interests of the health,
> safety, and welfare of the general public and to establish
> an Advisory Committee on Consumer Affairs to advise
> the Office of Consumer Affairs in carrying out its duties
> and functions under this chapter.

To these ends, the ordinance forbids merchants from
engaging in unfair and deceptive trade practices, and gives
the OCA the powers of enforcement through use of sub-
poenas and cease-and-desist orders—authority seldom
delegated to consumer-protection agencies. In addition to
acting in an enforcement capacity, the OCA handles complaints on an individual basis, represents the best interests
of consumers before administrative and legislative bodies,
and plans and implements programs of consumer education. The goals are, first, to aid individual consumers, and
second, to take steps to prevent similar complaints from
occurring in the future.

Montgomery County's OCA is succeeding where other
consumer-help agencies have failed. One reason is the new
law, but another is the commitment shown by all staff
members to the cause of representing the consumer's
interest in day-to-day complaints as well as in regard to
larger consumer issues. Says Barbara Gregg, Executive
Director: "We're small enough, we're new enough, and
we are not typical bureaucrats. I think there is a sense of

purpose—the staff feels that we are moving. We have this sense of purpose and excitement about our work."

Ms. Gregg, a former OEO Neighborhood Legal Services lawyer, heads a diverse team of full- and part-time staff (which at the moment numbers fifteen). Five are professional investigators with prior experience in antipoverty work who have a close understanding of the ethnic populations within their jurisdiction and an ability to interpret and apply the law.

The Montgomery OCA recruits according to regular county hiring policies, but it is interesting to note that qualifications of principal importance are "a commitment to serve people and a proven ability at problem-solving." Most training is done on the job. Each investigator works with a part-time law student. Besides assignment of thirty-five new cases each week, staff members work on in-depth investigations, draft necessary preventive legislation, and help satisfy ever-increasing requests for public appearances.

Complaints by consumers in Montgomery County most often fall into three categories: automobile sales and services (defective repair or failure to honor warranties); housing (shoddy workmanship in home improvement, deceptive advertising, and poor maintenance); and retail sales (mostly directed at appliance stores for defective products and failure to deliver). Lesser but still substantial complaints have been received about credit, food, drug, furniture, and clothing stores, door-to-door solicitations, government agencies, magazine-subscription services, and correspondence/career schools.

In a study of odometer rollbacks, three teams of investigators were sent out to check as many car dealers and automobiles as they could in one morning. They were instructed to examine frontline low-mileage cars, and to note both serial number and odometer reading. Some

100 vehicles were inspected at two thirds of the new-car dealers in the county. The information obtained was forwarded to the Maryland Department of Motor Vehicles, which in turn gave to the OCA the names of all former owners. Odometer rollbacks were discovered in six cases (three of which yielded sufficient evidence for referral to the county attorney for prosecution). Ms. Gregg appeared on television and radio to alert consumers to the possibility of odometer rollbacks and to describe what to look for in used cars with low mileage but signs of wear.

Besides referring cases to the county attorney and submitting legislation to the Maryland General Assembly, the Montgomery County OCA has prepared numerous educational materials, arranged for many lectures to business and citizen groups, as well as appearances on television, and in biweekly consumer radio shows. Staff members have also testified before federal agencies on proposed regulations, and before two neighboring county governments on the licensing of automotive mechanics and the feasibility of local consumer-protection agencies.

Currently under way are plans to reach low-income consumers and to disclose more specific information concerning merchants with a high volume of complaints. One of the OCA's priorities is to develop new ways to measure its effectiveness. But finding the criteria by which to judge the impact of any program is as difficult as it is important. "We want to measure our success in both handling individual complaints and formulating preventive programs," says Ms. Gregg. "It continually amazes us that we are one of the best consumer-protection agencies at the local level of government—but I think we are all very willing to admit that we are far from where we want to be."

While Congress wrestles with the question of establishing an independent Consumer Protection Agency, in certain parts of New York and Maryland the welfare of consumers is already paramount. Nassau County's OCA is "not here just to resolve complaints, but to resolve the problems that cause complaints." Barbara Gregg of Montgomery County claims her office "won't hesitate to use the full power we have to protect the consumer." In both places that's enough power to get some results.

The Court System

Courts at all levels today are plagued by heavy case loads, long delays, high costs, and sticky administrative problems. One effort toward reform—the Omnibus Hearing Procedure—was put into practice in 1967 by U.S. District Courts in San Antonio and San Diego. About two years ago the program was implemented in Jacksonville.

In omnibus hearings, criminal issues—normally raised only at the trial—are fully explored beforehand by way of a formal pretrial conference, in open court, in a manner similar to that suggested by the Federal Rules of Civil Procedure. Discovery of evidence is accomplished through voluntary disclosure of information by the prosecution and the defense, with the court ruling on a list of standard motions at a single hearing. Four features distinguish the omnibus hearing from existing practices:

—It brings together all of the actions required prior to trial, saving all parties time, energy, and other resources.

—It requires a routine exploration of claims customarily available to an accused, utilizing a checklist to insure that no claims remain unexposed.

—It allows customary claims to be raised and considered, as far as possible, without the preparation and filing of papers which so frequently perform no useful function in the proceedings.

—It provides that available claims be asserted or considered waived.

The omnibus discovery procedure thus eliminates the practice of written motions, provides a checklist, suggesting to defense counsel various procedures and tools available, secures unimpeded discovery by the prosecutor and the defense, and encourages voluntary disclosure by the prosecution. In addition, this procedure makes it possible to rule on requests for additional evidence, to dispose of latent constitutional issues, to provide a period of time prior to the omnibus hearing for disclosure of evidence so that a defendant can make an informed decision as to a plea of guilty, if such is his decision, and to postpone formal hearings on those matters which require preparation of written documents.

The omnibus procedure is entered into voluntarily by the interested parties and meets all standards set by the American Bar Association relating to pretrial discovery. This includes an exploratory phase, initiated by counsel and conducted without court supervision; the omnibus stage, where all matters are heard and determined under the supervision of the court; and a trial-planning period. The mechanics of the procedure are purposefully simple. The clerk's office determines the identity of defense counsel and mails him a letter containing information about the omnibus hearing, along with the assigned date of his client's arraignment. Lawyers advise the court and the United States Attorney in writing, within three days, whether or not they and their clients will participate. (It is assumed that the government will join if the defendant chooses the omnibus practice, unless advice to the contrary is given within three days.) If all counsel agree, a conference is held within ten days from the date of the clerk's original notice "for purposes of engaging in required discovery, entering upon plea discussions." An "Action Form" expedites matters: it is completed by circling paragraph numbers with respect to which action is requested.

At the time of arraignment (set far enough in advance to allow the full ten-day period to expire) the omnibus hearing is called—but only if one side or the other has indicated on the Action Form that one or more motions are pending. The defendant is thus able to make an enlightened and intelligent plea when first called before the court.

The San Antonio experience has been encouraging. Cases tried after the omnibus hearing procedure was instituted now require only a fraction of the time once needed, and they are presented in a more logical and understandable fashion. Though both defense and prosecuting attorneys were suspicious when the system was inaugurated two years ago, today both sides agree that there are many advantages. One lawyer has found it to be "a monumental time-saver, a great eliminator of paperwork and of useless sparring around with the United States Attorney, and an effective way to boil a case down to the critical issues in question." Another, a prosecutor, appreciates the added time he can spend briefing and researching more difficult and unique questions of law—which results in more pleas of guilty than he ever experienced before. (The latter is brought about by full disclosure of everything in the government's file to the defendant.)

Adrian A. Spears, Chief United States District Judge of San Antonio, says that "This venture proved to be a highly successful one from the start, primarily because of the fine spirit of cooperation manifested by attorneys for both the prosecution and the defense, who quickly realized that their clients' interests are much better served when their cases are well prepared and the element of surprise is minimized."

One of the harder tasks faced by a judge—indeed, one of the most difficult problems in the whole field of criminal law—is the sentencing of individuals convicted of crimes. Inequalities in sentencing strike at the very roots of the American heritage—"Equal Justice Under Law"—not only causing unfairness to the involved defendants but producing hardships for prison administrators in their rehabilitative programs. In the process, public respect for judges and their courts tends to diminish.

Though most courts are willing to devote unlimited time before and during trial in order to see "that justice prevails," they have been disinclined to expend similar effort in the equally important task of assessing penalty. Besides the complaints of those convicted, in the past few years legal scholars, penologists, legislators, and judges have expressed increased concern over an essential weakness in the judicial system: that which permits frequently disparate sentences to be handed down.

Statistics have shown substantial inconsistency in sentencing practices among certain federal districts. For example, the length of a term imposed for forgery varied from an average of four and a third years in one jurisdiction to only ten months in an adjoining one. For auto theft, an average of four-year sentences compared to that of fourteen months in adjacent districts. The defendants involved were frequently of similar age, background, and prior record.

There are numerous reasons which contribute to inconsistencies in sentencing. Chief among them are the wide latitude offered the sentencing authority in the selection of sanctions, the absence of established standards needed to measure the appropriateness of the dispositive actions, and the delegation of sentencing authority to one person. All of this tends to inhibit an important function of law; selection of an appropriate sentence is as critical to the admin-

istration of justice as the just determination of guilt. Its
effects extend far beyond the courtroom in which it is pro-
nounced; it has continuing repercussions on the defendant,
his family, and society.

In 1960, a U.S. District Court inaugurated a Judicial
Sentencing Council. Since that time other courts have followed their example. Its goals, as proposed by the Eastern
District Court of Michigan, were: 1) to provide an opportunity for several judges to appraise the same pre-sentence
information on a given offender, and 2) to develop among
its members a consensus in sentencing philosophy. Since
its inception in November 1960, approximately 10,000
criminal defendants have received the benefits of the group
approach to sentencing. Although it has been a time-consuming process for the judges involved, almost all of them
feel the time well spent.

A Sentencing Council is generally composed of three
judges, the chief or deputy chief probation officer, and one
other probation officer. A week prior to the Council meeting each participant is provided with a copy of the pre-
sentence investigative report which has been prepared for
the cases about to be considered. The pre-sentence report
includes information about the offense committed, the
defendant's version of the incident, his prior criminal
record, family history, marital background, home and
neighborhood, education, religion, interests, avocations,
physical and emotional health, employment, military service, and financial condition. Each Council member reads
the report and formulates an independent recommendation before the group convenes.

After reviewing this record the Council proceeds
(within statutory limits) to a consideration of the sentencing. Attending probation officers do not themselves
make recommendations but suggest a disposition to the
presiding judge. Cases are presented to the Council by the

judge before whom the defendant was convicted and by whom he will be sentenced. Normally each judge has five cases to be considered. He makes his comments and recommendations as to sentence and then requests the same from the other two judges and the probation officers present.

In practice the meetings have served to create a better understanding of goals to be sought in sentencing, facilities available for treatment of offenders, practices of the Bureau of Prisons, and policies of the local parole board. A correlative benefit is reflected in the opportunity for comparing sentences between defendants in two separate districts.

The Sentencing Council has served to demonstrate that when two or more judges review and appraise the same pre-sentence material on a given defendant, divergent opinions frequently result. After discussion, the same judges often gain a different appreciation of the case, and in many instances change their previous inclination to one conforming more closely to the consensus of the group.

The success of an undertaking of this nature depends in large measure upon the characteristics of its members: their humility, compatibility, and willingness to spend extra time and effort on individual cases. The judges of the Eastern District of Michigan appear to possess all three in sufficient measure to make that jurisdiction exemplary.

In Business and Labor

The Moving Men

Though all of them would agree that moving hearth and home is no picnic, one in four American families nevertheless relocates each year. They may wait days or weeks for a van, only to see cherished possessions damaged and be forced to hassle months on end to collect a fair amount on claims for losses. A *Consumer Reports* survey revealed that 25 per cent of families who moved from one state to another found serious fault with service and that, moreover, moving companies repeatedly broke the few Interstate Commerce Commission rules designed to help the public cope with an industry-oriented system of regulation.

The Movers' and Warehousemen's Association of Maryland, a trade group representing some fifty major moving and storage firms in Maryland, northern Virginia, and the District of Columbia, is a notable exception to this pattern of neglect. In 1969, the American Movers Conference had ranked the Maryland–D.C. area fourth among all states in volume of complaints received. Such poor public relations spurred the Maryland movers to devise a plan "to encourage and preserve public confidence in the advertising, selling, and performance of services." Since the resulting Registered Mover Program was put into operation, it has substantially reduced customer grievances—by means of fairly arbitrating their disputes with movers.

Under the program, a company must petition to become a Registered Mover. Only those firms with satisfactory consumer records—determined by the Better Business Bureau and the Maryland Attorney General's Consumer Protection Office—are eligible. As Registered Movers, the companies agree to: 1) follow the "Standards for Advertising and Selling Services of the Moving and Warehousing Industry," 2) arbitrate customer/mover disputes according to established procedures under the Registered Mover Program, 3) abide by the decision of the Arbitration Subcommittee, and 4) use the Registered Mover seal in all advertising.

When it first receives a complaint, the Movers' Association refers it to the Better Business Bureau; if the BBB cannot determine blame, the grievance is returned to the Association. The movers then attempt to arrange a settlement, short of arbitration. Should this fail, they select an arbitrator (from among representatives of moving companies not involved in the controversy). Both parties in the dispute may bring witnesses, photos, documents, and lawyers to the hearing. The arbitrator makes a decision (enforceable by the courts under a Maryland statute that has been adopted by other states). If the mover fails to comply within thirty days, he may be suspended—and ultimately expelled—from the Association.

Most cases are resolved without formal arbitration. In the three years since the Registered Mover Program was instituted, only four cases have gone as far as arbitration; about five per month are settled informally. Although the arbitrator's impartiality is open to question, experience has shown that the procedure usually works to the advantage of the consumer; the program would probably not work at all unless consumers felt they were being given a fair and impartial hearing.

The Movers' and Warehousemen's Association of Maryland has the only such grievance system in the country, wherein the movers themselves are pledged to accept binding arbitration.

In addition to its Registered Mover Program, the Association publishes tips on moving and storage, sends speakers to civic groups, and distributes pamphlets describing how consumers may redress their grievances, and the industry standards that have been implemented. As a result, complaints about movers received by the Baltimore BBB have been cut in half over the past two years.

The Retailers: Appliance Dealers

Since April 1970, the Major Appliance Action Panel has been an unusually effective ally for consumers with complaints against manufacturers or dealers. The Panel was an outgrowth of recommendations made by a Presidential task force, appointed in 1969 to investigate appliance warranties and servicing. The committee's initial report had proposed changes in manufacturing, marketing, and servicing of major home appliances, called for an improved system to handle complaints—and suggested the industry be given a year to institute voluntary action. If considerable progress were not made within that time, the task force recommended legislative remedies.

The Panel's activities are sponsored by manufacturers and retailers of major home appliances, including trash compactors, dehumidifiers, dishwashers, garbage disposers, gas incinerators, home laundry equipment, ranges, refrigerators, freezers, room air conditioners, and water heaters. Complaints received on other products (such as televisions, automobiles, and central air-conditioning systems) are referred to other appropriate trade groups. The three primary Panel sponsors—the Association of Home Appliance Manufacturers, the Gas Appliance Manufacturers Association, and the National Retail Merchants Association—pay the Panel's travel expenses and the salaries of a small permanent staff, but the seven Panel members serve without pay. The Panel meets every four to six weeks for two days, during which it devotes about two thirds of its time to reviewing individual complaints and seeking just solutions to them. The remainder of the time is spent on more general public relations: finding ways to make consumers aware of the group's existence, and reducing the areas of likely consumer-manufacturer conflict.

The Panel's broadest objectives are to represent consumer views and to counsel the industry so that its customer relations may be carried out with integrity. Particular attention was directed to the satisfactory handling of individual consumer complaints. The Panel was asked to make recommendations on grievance procedures, warranties, service and repair, and communications between the industry and consumers. Its procedure for handling complaints involves breaking stalemates through effective communication (promptly and with the right people), and thorough evaluation of each claim. Good faith by both parties is assumed.

In its first two years, the Panel processed over 5000 complaints. Seventy-four per cent were quickly satisfied, and most of the remainder were placed in a pending status; only 3 per cent were found to have no merit. Of the resolved grievances, 96 per cent were completed by effective communication (before detailed evaluation was required). Most complaints center on incompetent or slow service, delays in obtaining parts, and the high cost of repairs. Other problems frequently mentioned are unfair treatment or being ignored by a dealer or manufacturer and repeated failures of the same part.

The Panel has completed several studies in fulfilling its function of advising the industry. An Appliance Service Study found that most dealers blame inadequate compensation for in-warranty repairs, and this discourages them from rendering good service. In addition, keen sales competition leads to markups too low to allow for adequate servicing. (For their part, consumers must be educated to include repair costs in the total appliance ownership costs and to buy accordingly.) A Warranty Study measured (through analysis of seventy warranties) compliance with the industry's own guidelines on warranty content. Satisfactory compliance was found 75 per cent of the time; only ten warranties were judged to comply with all guidelines.

While settlement of complaints provides immediate benefit to individual consumers, the Panel's recommendations to industry can provide long-term and widespread benefits. To this end the group issues numerous press releases, makes available a warranty teaching kit, and publishes a "Handbook for the Informed Consumer."

The Retailers: Cooperators

In the San Francisco Bay Area, cooperative markets have been significant competitors for the public's patronage for some time. With good reason: nowhere else in the supermarket industry has a "chain" of food stores been so oriented toward protection of the consumer.

The Consumers Cooperative of Berkeley is the country's largest and perhaps most successful venture in group food shopping. Founded in 1936 as a small club of people interested in getting the greatest value for their money, the Berkeley Co-ops now boast 74,000 families, which account for a third of the city's grocery business.

In appearance the Berkeley cooperatives—which include besides a health food store and general markets an auto-repair garage, three gas stations, four pharmacies a hardware-variety store, and four "wilderness shops"—resemble their conventional mercantile counterparts. But beneath the surface are many people-related activities and a good deal of consumer-minded enterprise. Instead of being owned by shareholders dispersed over a wide area, the various stores belong to consumers who live in the community and who buy in them regularly. The cooperatives are in business primarily to serve their members. "Member families have gradually built a low-key empire of integrity," says *The Christian Science Monitor*, "verging on a way of life above and beyond the price of bread or dog food."

Co-op members run their own organization through an annually elected board of directors, which in turn hires and oversees day-to-day management personnel. Each consumer has one vote regardless of the number of shares held. The directors, all of whom serve without compensation, set policy which is subject to bylaws that have been approved by the membership (which is welcome to attend board meetings).

Anyone can become a Co-op member by paying a one-dollar registration fee and buying one or more membership shares (currently $5 each). Buyers are not considered active or "fair-share" members, however, unless they spend at least $100 for goods or services during the fiscal year, or own at least $50 in shares, or purchase at least one $5 share during the fiscal year. Investment in the Co-op may likewise be made through purchase of certificates of interest. Shopping at the cooperative stores is open to anyone, but only members can vote in board elections and on bylaw changes, and many of the ongoing community and consumer programs are restricted to members.

Food prices at the Co-ops are not in every instance lower than at conventional supermarkets, but they are always competitive. Quality and consistency are given prime consideration, as is fairness in merchandising. Employees are given to understand, for example, that it is not fair to the shopper to flash what looks like a lower price on an item by reducing the weight a half-pound. In other words, the consumer has a right to know exactly what he is paying.

Thus in Co-op markets there are few flashy banners, or impulse items like candy at the checkout stands. Meats are trimmed so that there is a minimum of waste—no tricky labeling or seductive lighting. All along the shelves there are signs which offer information about ingredients, hints on preparation, even criticism of name-brand products. (Read one placard in the orange-drink section: "Tang may be handy when camping. We do not recommend it for regular use. Co-op frozen orange juice is a true food while Tang is sugar plus chemicals. Their prices—quart for quart—are surprisingly close.")

The Co-op label is owned and controlled by the consumer cooperatives of the United States which include, besides the Berkeley stores, successful ventures in Illinois, Ohio, New York, Maryland, a small chain in New England, and a large one in Puerto Rico. Most of the items are made to Co-op's specifications by established suppliers (which also make national brands) ; quality is claimed to be at least as good and in some instances better—"We think better than the supermarkets' house brands," says one Co-op official.

All items are unit-priced (there are no "three for 49 cents" offers), and specials are clearly marked. A long sign along one wall lists alphabetically the locations of product types—à la most supermarkets—but there is also a prominently displayed "basic buys" section which relates to the four main food groups. No smoking is permitted in the food areas; in some stores cartons of cigarettes are kept out of view and must be requested for sale.

"You might save a little bit, you might not," says the official. "But in the long run we figure you'll never pay more, and you get a whole lot of extra services which other markets don't have." Indeed, besides supplying goods the Co-ops and their affiliated agencies provide credit, insurance, legal assistance services, books, and recreation. Unusual features in most stores include:

—A professional home economist to help shoppers with meal planning, food preparation, nutritional information and advice.

—Suggestion boxes and a hot line to the central Co-op offices which may be used at any hour of the day or night to register complaints—or compliments.

—"Kiddie Korrals," specially designed and equipped

child-care rooms where parents may leave their preschool
children for supervised, creative play at a nominal, and
voluntary, fee.

—Paperback-book exchanges, a device for accepting
used paperbacks as donations and making them available
(at 10 cents per book) for others to read (proceeds are
used for scholarships and member projects).

—Bulletin boards, providing free space for posters and
notices, as well as areas for advertising community services and personal items up for trade.

—Public-forum tables, to help citizens who wish to
communicate peaceably with one another on noncommercial public issues.

The Co-op also publishes a weekly newspaper, which
goes to all members and to many public officials and community organizations. An education department is responsible for bringing consumer issues to the attention of
members and nonmembers alike. In addition, members are
entitled to a discount on subscriptions to *Consumer Reports*,
a furniture sales-referral service, and meeting rooms. All Co-
op stores also contain public restrooms, accommodations not
normally found in supermarkets.

Members sometimes receive "patronage refunds" at the
end of the fiscal year, besides conventional dividends on
their shares. Although the Berkeley Co-ops do not always
turn a profit, they do always think of the consumer and
the community first. A number of members feel that there
should be more hard-nosed business principles applied, but
there is no denying what makes the Co-ops popular.
"Shopper loyalty," says a staff member, "is based on our
willingness to change and our efforts to counter the convenience food policy." "It's not the size of the dividend
or the refund that's important," says another, "but that

the shopper, by shopping, is supporting the idea of a co-op."

Not only customers but employees as well are educated to Co-op principles. "Many employees here started with the supermarket chains," remarks a home economist, "and they have habits which revolve around the dollar being the only thing. But this is a consumer-owned business, and today we have a greater diversity of membership, all of whom are coming because they want us to level with them about food."

The Unions: Household Employees

Between 1960 and the present, the number of individuals employed as household workers dropped from 2,500,000 to 1,100,000. Most recent statistics show that over 50 per cent of all domestics are black; their median income is about $1400 per year; most receive no employee benefits and no paid sick leave or vacation; and they have no protective legislation such as workmen's or unemployment compensation. In addition, although employers are required by law to deduct Social Security from wages paid to household workers, many do not. As a result the domestics are deprived of substantial retirement benefits.

The question: Given such working conditions and the low image accorded their jobs by society (and by the workers themselves), why do over one million women remain so employed? The answer: They have no choice. The great majority of domestics have not completed a high-school education. They have had no opportunity to learn the technical skills required for most jobs available in today's labor market. But, nevertheless, most of them must work to earn money to support their children (more than 250,000 are heads of households) or to supplement their husband's low earnings.

In 1964 and 1965, under the auspices of the Women's Bureau of the U.S. Department of Labor, representatives of some national voluntary organizations and governmental agencies were brought together to discuss what could be done to improve the working conditions of household domestics, and how to elevate their socioeconomic status. Thus was formed the National Committee on

Household Employment, a private, nonprofit group based in Washington, D.C.

Over twenty voluntary organizations participate in the NCHE, which is the only national body concerned exclusively with the problems of household employees. Before the Committee was created, household workers held an exceptionally weak position as a bargaining force because of the isolated circumstances in which they labor. Individual workers feared that attempts to improve working conditions through concerted action would cost them their jobs; few of them could afford the risk.

The goals of the NCHE are straightforward: to raise household wages at least to the minimum set forth by the Fair Labor Standards Act; to provide for paid vacations and holidays, sick leave and unemployment compensation; and to create among the workers, and their employers, an awareness of the value of their labor. To these ends the NCHE promoted pilot training programs, which include courses in modern home-management techniques. Participants were recruited by field offices through public-service announcements. They are counseled, trained, and placed in reasonably well-paying jobs. Good relations with the press helped get the word around.

The NCHE has developed materials which were used in its own training program, as well as in those conducted by vocational and educational organizations in many other states. At present, the Committee is trying to organize household workers into local self-help groups affiliated with the national body. There are now thirty-five such affiliates, including the In-Migrant Homemaker Training Program of the Women's Service Club (Boston, Massachusetts), which recruits immigrants with no employment training and trains them to become efficient homemaker specialists. Housekeeping, nutrition, grooming, and family care are among the skills taught. Another is Services United for Responsible and

Gainful Employment (Alexandria, Virginia), which recruits and trains individuals in every aspect of household employment, including invalid and child care. After graduation the agency hires the graduates as employees—with teams working together in apartments and private homes.

The NCHE currently receives general support from the Ford Foundation. The hope is that the workers themselves will eventually take over and establish their own local organizations to carry out many of the same functions. (A fledgling group called the Household Technicians of America—self-supporting, self-administered, and lobby-oriented, has already been established.)

The NCHE feels that it is especially important to establish a "Code of Standards" to which both the employee and employer would subscribe. The proposed code provides for such things as:

—Social Security. Earnings should be reported and payments made in accordance with the law for Social Security credit toward old age, survivors' and disability insurance.

—Sick Leave. Employees working one day a week in one home should receive one day of paid sick leave a year. Full-time employees should receive a minimum of six days of paid sick leave annually.

—Vacations. Full-time workers should receive two weeks of paid vacation after one year of service. Employees working one day a week in one home should receive one day of paid leave for each six month period worked.

—Holidays. Live-in workers should receive an annual minimum of eight legal holidays, with pay. Full-time, live-out employees should receive the equivalent of six legal holidays with pay. A day-worker working one day a week in one home should receive one paid legal holiday a year, providing the holiday falls on one of her normal working days.

In addition, employees must be notified at least a week in advance or be compensated in full by the employer, if an employer does not require her services for the agreed-upon time. The employee has the responsibility of notifying her employers as soon as possible if she is unable to report to work. Promptness, integrity, and courtesy should be observed by both parties. Rest period, mealtimes, telephone privileges, and time out for private activities should be agreed upon in advance of employment. The proposed code also would require that efficient, safe, and workable appliances and cleaning aids be provided, and that they be used carefully.

The Unions: Chemical Workers

It was Ulysses S. Grant who said that "whatever there is of greatness in the United States is due to labor. The laborer is the author of all greatness and wealth. Without labor there would be no government, and no leading class, and nothing to preserve."

For many laborers the struggle is to preserve themselves. Out of every twenty modern American blue collar workers, one will contract a serious occupational disease or suffer a job-related injury. Despite that grim statistic, however, the history of corporate efforts to protect workers against industrial accidents and diseases reflects a consistent pattern of neglect, interrupted but occasionally by serious attempts to establish and enforce sound health and safety regulations.

The first line of defense against occupational hazards should be formed by the workers themselves, but it has not been. Even large unions lack safety engineers and doctors to monitor the work environment, or lawyers to draft effective rules and litigate workmen's compensation cases. Only the most obvious job-related dangers are mentioned in labor-management negotiations. Though the labor press reports news about safety developments, it performs few of its own investigations. The victims remain the rank and file, who know little of the dangers they are exposed to each day and seldom possess the skills necessary to detect job hazards and develop positive strategies for prevention.

A notable exception to these various failures is the comprehensive health and safety program of the Oil, Chemical, and Atomic Workers International Union. As a result of employee education, contract negotiations, plant monitoring, research, legislation, and publicity—as well as professional and political support from its international offices —the OCAW has become a model of responsible self-help action.

One case in point ocurred in Pennsylvania, where employees at a beryllium plant agreed to join the OCAW in return for a commitment that the union would address itself, first and foremost, to local health problems. Until this time the company and its doctors had denied any health hazards associated with beryllium. The OCAW called in an expert on the disease, and she in turn had access to other specialists—engineers, scientists, and doctors—with whom she teamed up to determine the nature and seriousness of the problem at hand. Workers were sent to Boston for lung examinations, after which the cooperating doctors from Massachusetts General put the hospital's equipment into a U-Haul and returned to Pennsylvania, where a more definitive test for beryllium disease was conducted. The doctors delivered a depressing verdict: merely from breathing beryllium a number of men would develop the debilitating disease berylliosis. But as a direct result of union efforts, the company was prodded into beginning to clean up its operations.

Because of its experience with the occupational-health dilemma over the past several years, the OCAW created its own occupational-health department. The activities of the health and safety office are broken down into several categories: basic research into the health effects of various exposures to toxic materials and working conditions, an educational program for union members and interested laymen, and interaction with government and the professional community. Concerned with the effects of heavy metals (specifically lead and mercury), the OCAW purchased an atomic absorption spectrometer and placed it at

the Polytechnic Institute of Brooklyn, where urinalyses
are conducted. The union also runs blood tests on workers
exposed to lead, and is doing studies of eye-hand coordination and other tests for subclinical effects of heavy-metal
exposure. The OCAW has student interns from the medical school and the graduate environmental hygiene program
at the University of Cincinnati's Kettering Laboratory
who spend between three to six months at union headquarters carrying out research, teaching, and gaining
broad practical experience in occupational health. The
OCAW is one of the few labor unions where a young professional can obtain such training while working with the
rank and file. As part of the union's educational program,
it is training selected workers to carry out lung function
tests. OCAW is very interested in the effects of noise. As
a part of the University of Cincinnati program, a young
woman with a master's degree in noise studies is conducting hearing tests, correlating noise-induced hearing loss
with the presence of certain diseases of stress, and is teaching select members to administer these tests themselves.

In addition to their basic research, the OCAW has distributed staff-written booklets on mercury and benzene
and several additional booklets are forthcoming on asbestos, lead, and carbon disulfide. They cover much technical
material, yet they are written in terms understandable
to the layman. The OCAW also produces *Lifelines*, a newsletter published monthly in the regular union newspaper
dealing solely with Occupational Health and Safety. The
union has three slide shows which cover lung diseases,
welding, and occupational skin diseases—each accompanied
by a taped script. They are made available to other unions
at cost.

The OCAW uses its professional resources and the sophistication of its membership in the legislative arena. Tony
Mazzocchi, the union's legislative director, helped prepare

testimony for hearings which established the Occupational Safety and Health Act of 1970. The workers themselves appeared on Capitol Hill; their litany of personal experiences on the job contributed greatly to the passage of the Act. Testimony is currently being offered on issues not properly or completely addressed in the original legislation.

Mazzocchi himself does not think statutory regulation can fully redress the wrongs perpetrated on workers. "I am not going to be disillusioned by the law's inadequacies. I don't think that it ever will work, because I don't think that the government will allow it to. But the fight to secure the law is important—it dramatizes the problems. And the fight to enforce the law properly enables the workers better to defend themselves. They have realized that, even with the law, things have not substantively changed. Occupational-health-and-safety problems can only be corrected at the point of production—and you only do this when you are equipped with the knowledge, and the militancy, to demand change. It simply won't happen any other way."

The OCAW's successes sometimes seem small in the face of problems which still exist, but the union remains enthusiastic. "We have won concessions from plants at the bargaining table," says Mazzocchi. "The recently concluded breakthrough with the oil industry is a classic example. But the biggest rewards come from seeing the guys get turned on. We always keep in mind that the only way to improve the workers' environments successfully is to get the workers to do it themselves."

The Unions: Automobile Workers

Beginning in 1957, after a select Senate Committee uncovered corruption and deceit in substantial parts of the
American union movement, labor acted to polish its tar-
nished image. The American Federation of Labor expelled
wayward members and adopted Ethical Practices Codes,
and the unions made a strong effort toward self-discipline
by way of impartial public review. Though both the
threat of expulsion and the promulgation of ethical codes
have had cleansing effects, the public review boards, still
few in number, have offered the brightest prospects for
true union democracy.

Traditionally, the judicial process in unions has been
badly tangled with political power. Those in office also
control most avenues of trial and appeal; complaints by the
rank and file often lead to little more than votes of confidence for the union leaders; issues are decided less by
democratic principles than by political expedience. Public
review boards offer a cogent means by which a portion of
union authority is vested in private citizens—in no way
connected with the organization—and by which unfair or
improper internal practices are inhibited. At the same
time, the public face of the labor movement is made more
attractive.

One major union to adopt a system of impartial review
is the United Auto Workers. The UAW's Public Review
Board has primary jurisdiction to deal with all matters
related to alleged violation of any AFL-CIO ethical practices. The Board also has the power to review various
appeals arising under procedures set forth in the UAW

Constitution. With the exception of certain issues related
to the processing of shop grievances and concerned with
official bargaining policy, virtually any subject of dispute
can be brought before the Review Board.

In *Stephen* v. *Local 92, UAW*, a union election was conducted on a day when only 18 of 170 employees were working. The Public Review Board refused to affirm the judgment exercised by the local officials which had resulted in
the disenfranchisement of 89 per cent of the membership.
Furthermore, the Board rejected the International Executive Board's compromise solution (to hold another election
on the petition of 50 per cent of the affected members),
holding that an undemocratic election is not made democratic by adoption of the expedient that the new election
be conditioned upon a petition.

The UAW's Public Review Board consists of seven members, each having been appointed to a two-year term and
all "impartial persons of good public repute, not working
under the jurisdiction of the UAW or employed by the
International, or any of its subordinate bodies." Appointments are made by the International Executive Board
and ratified by the Constitutional Convention, which meets
biennially. Although not required by its Constitution to do
so, the union has adopted a practice of filling vacancies only
from the list of candidates submitted by remaining members. There is no provision for removing a member from
office.

To insure financial independence, four times each year
the Board's funds are replenished by the International
Union in amounts required to bring the balance to $30,000.
Average expenditures are $60,000 per year. The Board
maintains its own offices and hires its own executive staff.

A UAW member who wishes to lodge a grievance against
any official union body follows the standard constitutional
route, successively petitioning the local, the International

President, and the International Executive Board. If he remains unsatisfied, he may appeal to the Public Review Board, or, if he chooses, to the UAW Constitutional Convention but not to both. The decision of the Board is final and binding.

Thus by the time the Board undertakes formal review of a matter it has been considered at least twice previously. A minimum of three Board members participate in each appeal proceeding. Parties in the dispute may request oral argument before the Board, although its scope is usually limited to consideration of the material already in the record. (Records, transcripts, and arguments of the parties are always submitted, in writing.) The Board's reluctance to accept new evidence during its review derives from its view that internal union disputes be resolved wherever possible within the union structure itself. When agreement on a decision has been reached, a written opinion is rendered and mailed to the interested parties, as well as to newspapers, libraries, and universities.

While not expressly covered by the constitutional provisions governing its jurisdiction, the Public Review Board operates as a complaint department, conciliation service, and inspection office. Communication and contact are made by letter, phone, or in person. The Board's full-time staff offers advice as to whether the matter can be submitted for resolution within the internal remedies system.

"Public review is not a substitute for democracy but an important procedural guarantee which aids every democratic tendency within a union," concludes an analysis of the UAW operation by the Center for Study of Democratic Institutions. "It is not a miraculous solution for all of the problems of bureaucracy in the labor movement, but it is a major step forward. If review were to spread to other unions, it would be an institutional reform of real significance for the ideal of the free society."

Why the system of internal remedies and public review has not been adopted by other unions is unclear. Inertia seems to be a factor. Without cries from within for reform, it is unlikely that the leadership will take public review seriously. Many of the rank and file still fear that the introduction of outsiders into union government results in a loss of control. Though it is now fifteen years old, the public-review concept remains in its infancy compared to the strongly entrenched traditions and conservative nature of established, organized labor.

The Unions: Coalminers

It was something more than a symbolic gesture when the newly elected leadership of the United Mine Workers decided to hold an "end-of-an-era clearance sale" of the Cadillacs purchased by deposed union president Tony Boyle. The limousine auction was by sealed bid—open only to coal miners. The rank and file was finally back in the driver's seat.

By mid-December 1972, when a group calling itself Miners for Democracy succeeded in defeating Boyle's incumbent regime, it was not difficult to recognize the events of the last three years in the mining area as extraordinary. "The most important reform breakthrough in postwar American labor history," said the *Philadelphia Inquirer*; the *Denver Post* called it "a landmark." Few who lived through that period in mining history would dismiss the bitter fight for control of the UMW as a power struggle between the ins and outs. The war waged by the Miners for Democracy was a crusade against corruption, a desperate drive for protection against fatal disease, and a ringing summons for the rank and file to press for safety regulations to forestall another catastrophic accident.

For fifty years, true democracy within the United Mine Workers' Union had been suppressed—partially by John L. Lewis, whose powers of sarcasm and derision often were enough to shatter efforts at internal reform. During his tenure, various labor analysts came to suggest that democracy was not necessary for effective unionism, and might even be an obstacle: Though labor leaders might trample malcontents, the theory went, they get results for the workers, and that's what the movement is all about. But the union leadership came to view voting and pension rights as the playthings of idealogues and radical elitists. The UMW, once a model of enlightenment in American labor, ceased to protect its members even from death in the mines. When their power was challenged, at least some of Boyle's hierarchy were prepared to commit murder.

Miners for Democracy was born in 1969, when Joseph Yablonski first announced his candidacy against Boyle. Other labor leaders scoffed (George Meany shrugged it off as an attempt "by a kitchen boy to move into the dining room"). But Yablonski was more than an aspiring unionizer; he was leading a fight by rank and file activists— men who were ready to face vilification, blacklisting, even possible death, for the cause of social justice. In the process of his candidacy, more was accomplished than simply exposing union corruption: something was learned about the nature of reform movements, what motivates them, the risks to life and property that are encountered.

Yablonski was murdered in December 1969. But the rebel miners, with help from a few outside liberals, some talented attorneys and dedicated university students, a congressman, and one experienced labor staff man, carried on. Wildcat strikes by the rank and file closed West Virginia mines in support of new safety legislation; hundreds of men from the mines went to Washington, D.C. for mass lobbying. Where the union had most noticeably failed, the insurgents established new organizations: the Black Lung Association, the Association of Disabled Miners and Widows, the Miners Project. They also began publishing a rank and file newsletter, *The Miner's Voice*.

From 1960 to 1972, the miners had fought without the support of other unions, which remained distressingly aloof. The man chosen by a convention of 450 miners from across the coal fields to run against Boyle in a court-

ordered election wasn't given much more chance of winning than Yablonski. But Arnold Miller, a 49-year-old
miner himself, traveled across Appalachia to meet the men
in the fields, in the bathhouses where they shower, at their
homes. "Under my leadership," Miller said to them, "coal
will be mined safely or not at all." All told, Miller visited
more than 200 mine sites. Instead of campaigning solely
on the issue of UMW corruption, he talked long and hard
about the need for such things as sick-pay benefits: they
work in the most dangerous and unhealthy of any major
industry, but coal miners who miss a day of work miss
a day's pay.

Miners for Democracy won a court order forcing the
UMW Journal to publicize his appeal for a nation-wide
drive to rebuild the miners' Welfare and Retirement Fund,
which gets its money from royalties on every ton of UMW
coal mined.

Three years after Yablonski's death the movement he
had launched succeeded in toppling an almost invincibly
entrenched power structure. The vote was overwhelming.
After the brief euphoria of election victory began the
grueling, everyday job of restoring a union which had
become tragically corrupt and had increasingly failed its
rank and file members.

At stake were the lives of 200,000 coal miners, their
families, and their communities. "I saw a lot of sick men
in this campaign," said Miller, "men who choked when
they tried to breathe, who had stumps where their legs
should have been. I shook a lot of hands that had missing
fingers. There's been too much blood on the coal. It's
going to stop." Miller expanded the union's safety division
to include mining engineers, doctors, lawyers, and rank
and file miners who know the safety problems first-hand.
He called for a team to travel the coal fields making unan-
nounced inspections, and shutting down unsafe mines. It

is clear that the new leadership will assume an adversary role with government agencies—particularly the U.S. Bureau of Mines, which recently said it was now safer to mine coal than to drive a car on the highways.

Miners for Democracy are proving that their campaign platform was more than promises. Miller rejected any accommodation with the self-chosen remnants of the Boyle machine. The new board cut top officers' salaries by 25 to 30 per cent and abolished automatic expense accounts. Boyle's pension was reduced from $50,000 to $16,000 a year. About $2 million in assorted savings was returned to the union treasury, part of which will go to raise the wages of the union's custodial staff—some of whom were getting only $100 per week.

In addition, Miller advocated that the coal companies renegotiate grievance procedures, which in the past have been so cumbersome that a coal miner was often fired before he won a justified complaint. The union has initiated a national credit union so that miners in isolated Appalachian towns can obtain credit at lower interest rates. The UMW's safety department has greatly expanded in size and scope. The occupational-health department, in cooperation with the Appalachian Regional Commission, is supplying sophisticated equipment to eight clinics in an effort to detect coal-dust respiratory diseases in their early stages. Detailed procedures for handling all financial transactions have been implemented. Union employees have been given free access to the elected leadership. The legislative department is developing a broad range of programs from backing liberal legislation in Congress to supporting the election of local candidates.

Stolen elections, corruption, mishandling of pension money, the initial failure of the Labor Department to enforce the law—that part of the miners' experience is still the plight of other unionists. Though the election success of the Miners for Democracy, exhilarating as it was, cannot directly affect events elsewhere, union reformers will surely be encouraged to carry on.

Although the situation at Boyle's UMW had been a unique dark age of murder, corruption, unresponsiveness to health and safety issues, now, for the first time in recent history, rank and file union members were able to topple entrenched leaders. The moral atmosphere in the labor movement has been noticeably freshened. "Stay close to the men," one miner told Miller after he had won the presidency. It looks as if he will.